# THE WASHINGTON NATIONAL MALL

PETER R. PENCZER · ONEONTA PRESS

D1497293

## Acknowledgments

This book is dedicated to my parents, Peter and Lynne Penczer, without whose encouragement and support it would not have been possible.

Special thanks go to James M. Goode, who reviewed the manuscript several times and helped in innumerable other ways, and to Matthew Gilmore, who carefully reviewed the manuscript and provided data for the maps on pages 58 and 110.

My thanks and deep appreciation also go to Antoinette J. Lee, Edith Levine, Madeline Li, Tony Simon, and my parents, who read the manuscript and made many valuable suggestions. I am equally grateful to William C. Allen, Sue A. Kohler, Priscilla W. McNeil, John Parsons, and John M. Woodbridge, who answered my questions and provided many useful comments on the manuscript. Dana Dalrymple generously supplied much of the information on the Department of Agriculture, and I am most appreciative.

My thanks also go to Charles Atherton, Don Alexander Hawkins, Stephen Potter, Gary Scott, and Pamela Scott, who answered many questions and were always generous with their time. I would like to express my gratitude to the staffs of the Historical Society of Washington, D.C.; the Washingtoniana Division of the D.C. Public Library; the Kiplinger Washington Collection; the Prints and Photographs Division of the Library of Congress; and the National Archives, for the many hours they spent assisting me as I researched this book. I am also grateful to Albert H. Small, Robert A. Truax, and Chevy Chase Bank for their generosity in permitting me to use their collections.

Finally, my thanks go to Jayson Hait, for copyediting the manuscript, and to Robert L. Wiser, for designing the page layout and typography.

Oneonta Press
Arlington, Virginia
www.dchistory.com

The Washington National Mall
ISBN 0-9629841-2-4 (pb); ISBN 0-9629841-3-2 (hc)
Library of Congress Control Number: 2005909397

# TABLE OF CONTENTS

Detail of the John Paul Jones Memorial

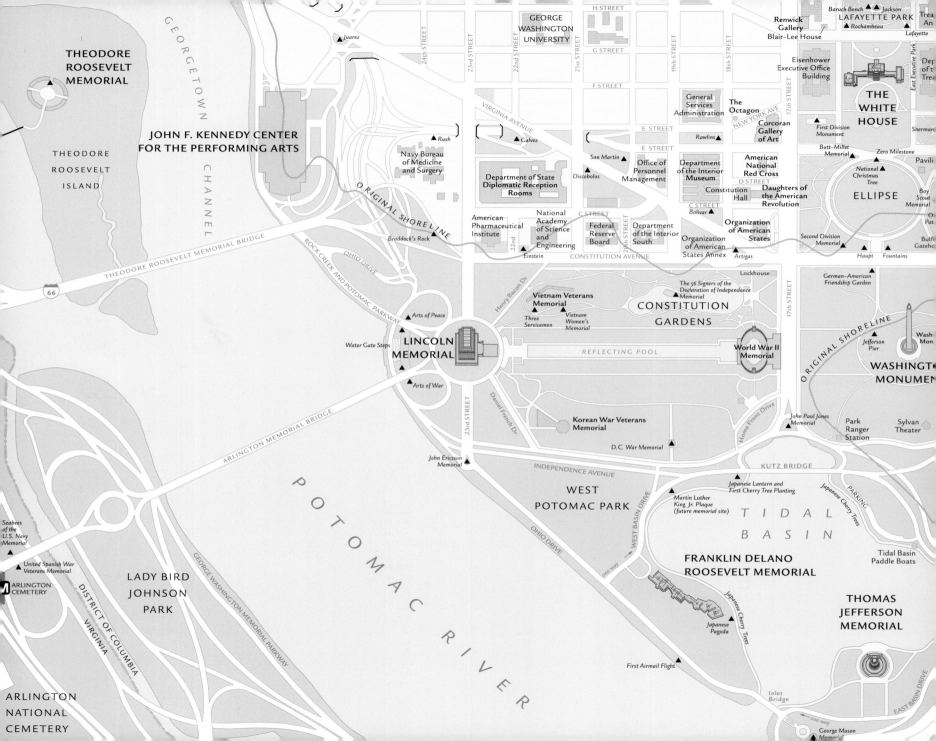

THEODORE
ROOSEVELT
MEMORIAL

▲

THEODORE
ROOSEVELT
ISLAND

GEORGETOWN CHANNEL

JOHN F. KENNEDY CENTER
FOR THE PERFORMING ARTS

*Juarez* ▲

H STREET

GEORGE
WASHINGTON
UNIVERSITY

24th STREET

23rd STREET

22nd STREET

21st STREET

G STREET

F STREET

VIRGINIA AVENUE

*Rush* ▲

E STREET

*Galvez* ▲

Navy Bureau
of Medicine
and Surgery

Department of State
Diplomatic Reception
Rooms

*Discobolus* ▲

E STREET

*San Martin* ▲

General
Services
Administration

The
Octagon

*Rawlins* ▲

Office of
Personnel
Management

Department
of the Interior
Museum

NEW YORK AVE

Corcoran
Gallery
of Art

American
National
Red Cross

20th STREET

19th STREET

18th STREET

17th STREET

Renwick
Gallery

Blair–Lee House

Baruch Bench ▲  ▲ Jackson
LAFAYETTE PARK
▲ Rochambeau

*Lafayette* ▲

Eisenhower
Executive Office
Building

East Exec Park

Tree
An

Dep
of t
Tre

THE
WHITE
HOUSE

First Division
Monument

Butt–Millet
Memorial

Sherman

Zero Milestone

Pavili

C STREET

American
Pharmaceutical
Institute

National
Academy
of Science
and
Engineering

*Einstein* ▲

C STREET

Federal
Reserve
Board

22nd

26th STREET

Department
of the Interior
South

CONSTITUTION AVENUE

Constitution
Hall

Daughters of
the American
Revolution

D STREET

C STREET

Organization
of American
States

Organization
of American
States Annex

*Artigas* ▲

*Bolivar* ▲

National
Christmas
Tree

Second Division
Memorial

ELLIPSE

*Haupt* ▲

Boy
Scout
Memorial

Fountains

Bulfi
Gateho

▲

O RIGINAL SHORELINE

THEODORE ROOSEVELT MEMORIAL BRIDGE

66

ROCK CREEK AND POTOMAC PARKWAY

OHIO DRIVE

*Braddock's Rock* ▲

Henry Bacon Dr

Arts of Peace ▲

LINCOLN
MEMORIAL

Water Gate Steps

Arts of War ▲

Vietnam Veterans
Memorial

*Three
Servicemen* ▲

Vietnam
Women's
Memorial ▲

The 56 Signers of the
Declaration of Independence
Memorial

CONSTITUTION
GARDENS

REFLECTING POOL

Lockhouse

World War II
Memorial

O RIGINAL SHORELINE

17th STREET

German–American
Friendship Garden

Jefferson
Pier ▲

Wash
Mon

▲

WASHINGTO
MONUMEN

ARLINGTON MEMORIAL BRIDGE

23rd STREET

Daniel French Dr

Korean War Veterans
Memorial

D.C. War Memorial ▲

John Ericsson
Memorial ▲

Home Front Drive

INDEPENDENCE AVENUE

John Paul Jones
Memorial ▲

Park
Ranger
Station

Sylvan
Theater

KUTZ BRIDGE

POTOMAC RIVER

Seabees
of the
U.S. Navy
Memorial ▲

United Spanish War
Veterans Memorial ▲

ARLINGTON
CEMETERY

LADY BIRD
JOHNSON
PARK

GEORGE WASHINGTON MEMORIAL PARKWAY

DISTRICT OF COLUMBIA
VIRGINIA

WEST
POTOMAC PARK

WEST BASIN DRIVE

OHIO DRIVE

one-way

Japanese Lantern and
First Cherry Tree Planting ▲

Martin Luther
King Jr. Plaque
(future memorial site) ▲

FRANKLIN DELANO
ROOSEVELT MEMORIAL

Japanese Cherry Trees

Japanese
Pagoda ▲

Japanese Cherry Trees ▲

TIDAL
BASIN

PARKING

THOMAS
JEFFERSON
MEMORIAL

Tidal Basin
Paddle Boats

First Airmail Flight ▲

Inlet
Bridge

EAST BASIN DRIVE

one-way

George Mason
Memorial ▲

ARLINGTON
NATIONAL
CEMETERY

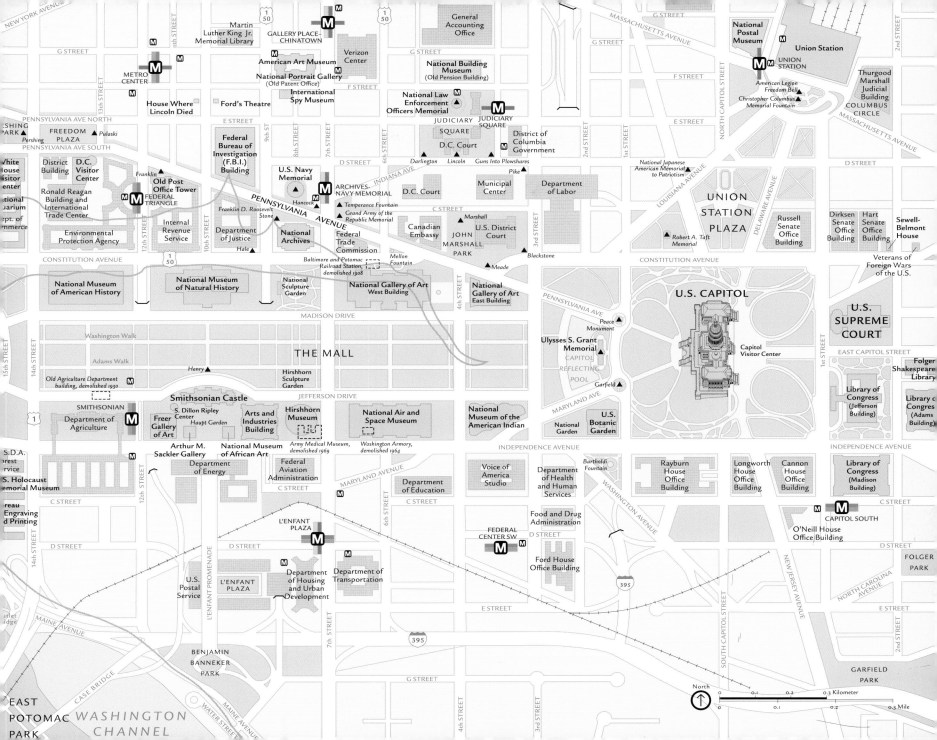

NEW YORK AVENUE

G STREET

Martin Luther King Jr. Memorial Library

GALLERY PLACE-CHINATOWN

General Accounting Office

G STREET

MASSACHUSETTS AVENUE

G STREET

National Postal Museum

Union Station

METRO CENTER

American Art Museum

National Portrait Gallery
(Old Patent Office)

Verizon Center

UNION STATION

American Legion Freedom Bell

Thurgood Marshall Judicial Building

House Where Lincoln Died

Ford's Theatre

F STREET

National Building Museum
(Old Pension Building)

F STREET

Christopher Columbus Memorial Fountain

COLUMBUS CIRCLE

International Spy Museum

National Law Enforcement Officers Memorial

E STREET

E STREET

MASSACHUSETTS AVENUE

WASHINGTON PARK

FREEDOM PLAZA ▲ Pulaski

Pershing

PENNSYLVANIA AVE NORTH

Federal Bureau of Investigation (F.B.I.) Building

JUDICIARY SQUARE

JUDICIARY SQUARE

PENNSYLVANIA AVE SOUTH

D.C. Court

District of Columbia Government

White House Visitor Center

District Building

D.C. Visitor Center

Old Post Office Tower

U.S. Navy Memorial

Darlington Lincoln Guns Into Plowshares

National Japanese American Memorial to Patriotism

Dirksen Senate Office Building

Hart Senate Office Building

Ronald Reagan Building and International Trade Center

FEDERAL TRIANGLE

Internal Revenue Service

Franklin

ARCHIVES-NAVY MEMORIAL

Hancock

Pike

D.C. Court

Municipal Center

Department of Labor

UNION STATION PLAZA

Sewell-Belmont House

Russell Senate Office Building

National Aquarium

Dept. of Commerce

Environmental Protection Agency

Department of Justice

Franklin D. Roosevelt Stone

Hale

National Archives

▲ Temperance Fountain

▲ Grand Army of the Republic Memorial

Federal Trade Commission

C STREET

Canadian Embassy

JOHN MARSHALL PARK

▲ Marshall

U.S. District Court

▲ Robert A. Taft Memorial

Veterans of Foreign Wars of the U.S.

CONSTITUTION AVENUE

Baltimore and Potomac Railroad Station, demolished 1908

Mellon Fountain

▲ Meade

Blackstone

CONSTITUTION AVENUE

National Museum of American History

National Museum of Natural History

National Sculpture Garden

National Gallery of Art West Building

National Gallery of Art East Building

U.S. CAPITOL

U.S. SUPREME COURT

MADISON DRIVE

PENNSYLVANIA AVE

Ulysses S. Grant Memorial

▲ Peace Monument

Capitol Visitor Center

EAST CAPITOL STREET

Washington Walk

THE MALL

CAPITOL REFLECTING POOL

Folger Shakespeare Library

Adams Walk

▲ Garfield

Library of Congress (Jefferson Building)

Library of Congress (Adams Building)

Old Agriculture Department building, demolished 1930

▲ Henry

Hirshhorn Sculpture Garden

JEFFERSON DRIVE

MARYLAND AVE

SMITHSONIAN

Smithsonian Castle

National Garden

U.S. Botanic Garden

Department of Agriculture

Freer Gallery of Art

S. Dillon Ripley Center

Haupt Garden

Arts and Industries Building

Hirshhorn Museum

National Air and Space Museum

National Museum of the American Indian

S.D.A. Forest Service

Arthur M. Sackler Gallery

National Museum of African Art

Army Medical Museum, demolished 1969

Washington Armory, demolished 1964

INDEPENDENCE AVENUE

INDEPENDENCE AVENUE

U.S. Holocaust Memorial Museum

Department of Energy

Federal Aviation Administration

Voice of America Studio

Department of Health and Human Services

Bartholdi Fountain

Rayburn House Office Building

Longworth House Office Building

Cannon House Office Building

Library of Congress (Madison Building)

C STREET

C STREET

C STREET

C STREET

Bureau of Engraving and Printing

U.S. Postal Service

L'ENFANT PLAZA

Department of Education

Food and Drug Administration

FEDERAL CENTER SW

CAPITOL SOUTH

O'Neill House Office Building

FOLGER PARK

L'ENFANT PLAZA

Department of Housing and Urban Development

Department of Transportation

Ford House Office Building

D STREET

D STREET

D STREET

D STREET

BENJAMIN BANNEKER PARK

E STREET

E STREET

EAST POTOMAC PARK

WASHINGTON CHANNEL

GARFIELD PARK

North

0 0.1 0.2 0.3 Kilometer

0 0.1 0.2 0.3 Mile

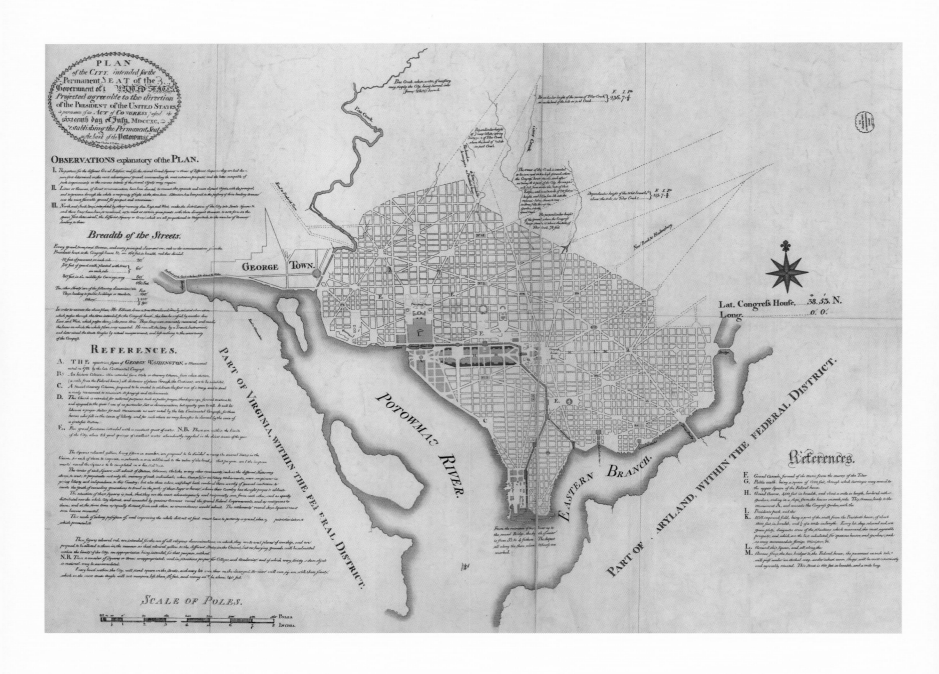

PLAN
of the CITY intended for the
Permanent SEAT of the
Government of t UNITED STATES
Projected agreeable to the direction
of the PRESIDENT of the UNITED STATES
in pursuance of an ACT of CONGRESS passed the
sixteenth day of July, MDCCXC,
establishing the Permanent Seat
on the bank of the Potowmac

OBSERVATIONS explanatory of the PLAN.

I. The positions for the different Grand Edifices, and for the several Grand Squares or Areas of different shapes as they are laid down, were first determined on the most advantageous ground, commanding the most extensive prospects, and the better susceptible of such improvements as the various intents of the several objects may require.

II. Lines or Avenues of direct communication have been devised to connect the separate and most distant objects with the principal, and to preserve through the whole a reciprocity of sight at the same time. Attention has been paid to the passing of those leading Avenues over the most favorable ground for prospect and convenience.

III. North and South lines intersected by others running due East and West, make the distribution of the City into Streets Squares &c. and those lines have been so combined, as to meet at certain given points with those divergent Avenues, so as to form on the spaces first determined, the different Squares or Areas, which are all proportional in Magnitude to the number of Avenues leading to them.

Breadth of the Streets.

Every Grand transversal Avenue, and every principal Avenue such as the communication from the President's house to the Congress house &c. are 160 feet in breadth, and thus divided:
10 feet of pavement on each side — 20
30 feet of gravel walk, planted with trees on each side — 60
80 feet in the middle for Carriage way — 80
160 feet
The other Streets are of the following dimensions viz.
Those leading to public buildings or markets — 130
Others — 110 / 90

REFERENCES.

A. THE equestrian figure of GEORGE WASHINGTON, a Monument voted in 1783 by the late Continental Congress.

B. An historic Column — Also intended for a Mile or itinerary Column, from whose station, (a mile from the Federal house) all distances of places through the Continent, are to be calculated.

C. A Naval itinerary Column, proposed to be erected to celebrate the first rise of a Navy, and to stand a ready Monument to consecrate its progress and achievements.

D. This Church is intended for national purposes, such as public prayer, thanksgivings, funeral orations &c. and assigned to the special use of no particular Sect or denomination, but equally open to all. It will be likewise a proper shelter for such monuments as were voted by the late Continental Congress, for those heroes who fell in the cause of liberty, and for such others as may hereafter be decreed by the voice of a grateful Nation.

E. Five grand fountains intended with a constant spout of water. N.B. There are within the limits of the City, above 25 good springs of excellent water abundantly supplied when in the driest season of the year.

PART OF VIRGINIA, WITHIN THE FEDERAL DISTRICT.

POTOWMAC RIVER.

EASTERN BRANCH.

PART OF MARYLAND, WITHIN THE FEDERAL DISTRICT.

GEORGE TOWN.

Lat. Congress House, 38. 53. N.
Long. 0. 0.

References.

F. Grand Cascade, formed of the water from the sources of the Tiber.

G. Public walk, being a square of 1200 feet, through which carriages may ascend to the upper Square of the Federal house.

H. Grand Avenue, 400 feet in breadth, and about a mile in length, bordered with Gardens, ending in a slope, from the house on each side. This Avenue leads to the Monument A. and connects the Congress garden, with the

I. President's park, and the

K. Well improved field, being a part of the walk from the President's house, of about 1800 feet in breadth, and 3/4 of a mile in length. Every lot deep colored red, was first proposed to be divided in the manner as the lots colored yellow below.

L. Around this Square, and all along the Avenue from the two bridges to the Federal house, the pavement on each side, will pass under an arched way, under what cover, shops will be most conveniently and agreeably situated. This Street is 160 feet in breadth, and a mile long.

M. [text continues]

SCALE OF POLES.

Poles.
Inches.

The National Mall is America's greatest urban park. It is the site of memorials to our most important national heroes and home to the Smithsonian Institution, the largest museum complex in the world. A broad greensward bordered by rows of elms, it stretches 2¼ miles from the Capitol to the Potomac River, between Constitution and Independence avenues.

The Mall was conceived in 1791 as part of Peter Charles L'Enfant's plan for the city of Washington. His precise plans for the Mall are unclear, but he probably intended a broad expanse of grass, bordered by trees and fine mansions. Nevertheless, the Mall remained essentially undeveloped until the late 1840s, when work began on the Washington Monument and the Smithsonian "Castle." Soon after, renowned landscape architect Andrew Jackson Downing completed a naturalistic landscaping plan for the Mall that featured winding paths and artfully scattered trees, but his untimely death prevented its full implementation.

In the 1870s, the Army Corps of Engineers completed the landscaping in the informal style of Downing, but their Mall was very different from the one we know today. It was densely planted with trees, and graveled carriage paths curved through the park. There were a number of elaborate Victorian buildings, all but a few of which have since been demolished.

In 1901, Senator James McMillan charged a small group of eminent American architects and artists with devising a plan for the improvement of the Mall. Inspired by the 1893 World's Columbian Exposition, they proposed rows of gleaming white buildings and formal, geometric landscaping. In the decades to follow, their plan was largely carried to completion. It was a radical transformation that required razing virtually every building and removing nearly every tree on the Mall. The McMillan Plan, as it became known, remains the guiding light for the development of Washington's monumental core.

OPPOSITE. The city of Washington was designed in 1791 by Peter Charles L'Enfant, a French-born engineer and architect. L'Enfant's original plan for the city, now at the Library of Congress, is in poor condition. This is a facsimile made in 1887 by the U.S. Coast and Geodetic Survey.

LEFT. Secretary of State Thomas Jefferson devised his own scheme for the city of Washington, a modest grid that would have been located north of present-day Constitution Avenue. It featured a broad open area along the Potomac labeled "public walks," which presaged L'Enfant's Mall. L'Enfant dismissed Jefferson's simple gridiron plan as "a mean continuance of some cool imagination" and persuaded Washington to accept his own, far grander, plan.[1]

RIGHT. A detail from L'Enfant's 1791 plan for the city shows the Mall (H.) lined with houses, here colored in red. The plan provided for an equestrian statue of Washington (A.) and a "grand cascade" of water (F.) issuing from the base of the Capitol.

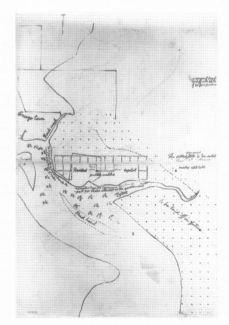

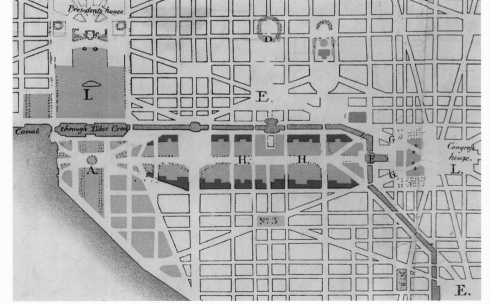

THE STORY OF THE MALL begins with the creation of Washington, the new capital of the young American nation. In July 1790, Congress passed the Residence Act, legislation authorizing a new federal city on the Potomac River. President George Washington was allowed to select the exact location and designate a federal district up to 10 miles square. He chose the confluence of the Potomac and the Anacostia rivers, the latter more commonly known as the Eastern Branch.

It was an attractive site, relatively flat and framed by navigable rivers on two sides and a ring of hills on the other. To design the new city, Washington engaged Peter Charles L'Enfant, a French-born engineer. L'Enfant had come to the United States to fight in the Revolutionary War and afterward settled in New York, where he worked as an architect. Washington knew L'Enfant from the war and had great respect for his abilities.

L'Enfant completed his plan in the summer of 1791 after a few months of work. His design had an unequally spaced grid of streets combined with diagonal avenues, resulting in many oddly shaped blocks. At important intersections there were public squares, and there were sites for important public buildings. It was a magnificent plan, enormous in scale and fit to be the capital of a great nation.

Vistas were important to L'Enfant, and he used the natural topography to advantage, placing the Capitol atop a hill, where it commanded a view across a broad open area to the Potomac River. The President's House was to be set atop a low ridge, more than a mile to the west, looking south across a park to the river. Where the vistas from the Capitol and the President's House intersected on the banks of the Potomac, he suggested locating an equestrian statue of Washington that had been authorized by Congress in 1783, but never realized. This would later be the site of the Washington Monument, the great obelisk begun in 1848.

The broad open area from the Capitol to the river would become the National Mall. L'Enfant described it on his plan for the city, with letters indicating the important landmarks: "H. Grand avenue 400 feet in breadth, and about a mile in length, bordered with gardens, ending in a slope from the houses on each side. This avenue leads to the [Washington] Monument A. and connects the Congress garden with the I. President's park." L'Enfant probably intended his "grand avenue" to be a grassy park, rather than a boulevard busy with traffic. In a letter to Washington, he described the Mall, writing that "the whole will acquire new sweetness being laid over the green of a field well level and made brilliant by shade of a few trees artfully planted."[2]

L'Enfant was inspired by the formal French landscaping of his day, but his precise influences are unknown. An obvious source were the gardens at Versailles, the city where he spent his youth. Another was the Place de la Concorde in Paris (then known as the Place Louis XV), a large square fronting on the Seine River that had an equestrian monument to Louis XV at its center. The resemblance is unmistakable: The arrangement of the monumental buildings and parks about the Mall corresponds precisely to the arrangement of the Madeleine Church, the Louvre, and the Tuileries Gardens around the Place de la Concorde.

In February 1792, President Washington fired L'Enfant because he refused to submit to the authority of the District's three commissioners, who oversaw the establishment of the city. L'Enfant was replaced by Andrew Ellicott, who had been hired the previous year to survey the boundaries and topography of the new federal district. Working with Secretary of State Thomas Jefferson, Ellicott made a number of changes to L'Enfant's plan and gave it a more precise and concrete form.

In a letter to the commissioners on January 4, 1793, seeking guidance on setting the precise width of the Mall, Ellicott referred to it as the "mall"[3]—a term that L'Enfant apparently did not use. The park was commonly called the "Mall" throughout the nineteenth century, although it was often referenced in public documents as the public grounds or the public reservations.

The word *mall* derives from *paille-maille*, a game that was played in seventeenth-century France but has long since disappeared. Similar to croquet, it was played with a mallet and a large wooden ball on a long alley. The game spread to England where it was known as pall-mall, and the alley, as a pall-mall or mall. *Mall* eventually came to mean any open promenade, including a promenade lined with shops, such as a modern shopping mall.

Sarah DeHart's silhouette of Peter Charles L'Enfant (1754–1825) was made about 1785 and is the only surviving image of L'Enfant taken from life.

This 1850 print by Robert P. Smith accurately depicts the Capitol as it appeared at that time, before the new wings and dome were added. Smith shows the Washington Monument as completed, although work had barely begun.

GEORGE WASHINGTON acquired the land for the new capital city through an agreement with the original proprietors, the planters who owned the roughly 6,000 acres covered by L'Enfant's plan for the city. In exchange for their land, the proprietors would receive half of the city lots and payment for any land taken for public purposes other than streets. There were about 30 proprietors, but Daniel Carroll of Duddington had the largest holdings, about 1,400 acres. His estate was named Cerne Abbey Manor.

Early land records are often cryptic, and historians have had difficulty determining where the various tracts of land were situated. Research by Priscilla McNeil shows that Carroll owned most of the land south of Tiber Creek, including the site of the Capitol and the Mall. The land that would become his estate was originally granted by King Charles I to Cecilius Calvert, the second Lord Baltimore, in 1632. He, in turn, patented three tracts to George Thompson in 1664. Thompson sold the tracts to Thomas Notley, who had them resurveyed into one combined tract, Cerne Abbey Manor. After Notley's death the land went to his godson Notley Rozer, and from Rozer, it descended through family members to Carroll.

In 1664, Francis Pope received a patent for a tract named Rome. McNeil's research suggests that Pope's land lay entirely within one of the tracts patented to George Thompson. Apparently, Pope never occupied his tract, and his patent was later abandoned. The name of Tiber Creek seems to have been a continuation of the pun

An 1839 watercolor by Augustus Köllner shows Tiber Creek north of the Capitol. In the background is Notley Young's mill, which stood near N and First streets, N.E.

L'Enfant laid out the city, but it is probable that it was open land, with dense foliage bordering the Tiber and the Potomac.[5] In 1866, Christian Hines gave the following account of the Tiber of his youth, more than 60 years earlier:

At this time there were still a considerable number of trees around and about the Capitol and creek, intermixed with grape vines, clumps of thorn bushes, etc., extending from the Capitol almost to Seventh Street bridge [over the Tiber]; in short, it was a complete little wilderness.[6]

In 1804, the city government passed an act establishing an agricultural fair that was to be held every May and November on the Mall between the Seventh Street bridge and the Potomac River, so this part of the Mall was undoubtedly clear of trees.[7] How long these fairs were held is unknown, but Christian Hines mentions one of the amusements there:

There was held a fair on the Mall on the south side of Tiber Creek, near the margin of the creek, but between it and where the Smithsonian Institution now stands … my impression is that it was not kept up very long. Some, who were fond of sport, would get two of the poorest looking and roughest horses they could find, and then get two of the worst looking men to ride them. They would then start them on a race, in front of the tents towards where the Washington Monument now stands, amidst laughter, shouting and harrahing.[8]

The slopes of Capitol Hill were more heavily wooded. A 1796 account by Thomas Twining described the unfinished Capitol as standing in a clearing in the woods, with the newly cleared avenues radiating outward like the spokes of a wheel.[9]

Archeological excavations on the Mall have been limited, and in any case, much of the original stratigraphy is deeply buried under landfill deposited in later years. The only American Indian artifact known to have been found in the park was described as a soapstone pestle, found on the grounds of the Washington Monument about 1875. It was deposited at the Smithsonian, but was later deaccessioned, and its present whereabouts are unknown.[10] At the time of European contact, the Piscataway tribe occupied the area that is now the District of Columbia. Early explorers recorded a number of villages in the area, but none in the vicinity of the Mall.

on Pope's name, since Tiber is also the name of a river that flows through Rome in Italy.[4]

When L'Enfant devised his plan for the city, the area was sparsely inhabited by planters and tenant farmers. The Mall was located on the north side of a short peninsula between Tiber Creek and the Potomac. The western tip of the peninsula, known as Mattingly's Point, would later be the site of the Washington Monument. Although its elevation above sea level was low, most of the Mall was high and dry. Only a small area, along Tiber Creek near the present-day East Building of the National Gallery of Art, was marshy. The popular notion that Washington was built on a swamp is a myth.

Tiber Creek, where it flowed along the north side of the Mall, was slow moving and broad, and its waters, like those of the Potomac, rose and fell with the tides. From the creek, the Mall sloped gradually uphill toward the south; consequently, the southern side of the Mall was higher and drier, and that is where the first buildings, such as the Smithsonian Castle, would be built. There are no contemporary descriptions of the Mall in the first decades after

ALTHOUGH CONGRESS first met at Washington in 1800, the Mall would remain unfinished for many years. A canal, a botanic garden, and some modest landscaping were the most important improvements to the Mall in the first decades of the nineteenth century. According to one account:

The Mall prior to 1850 [was] a large common stretching from Seventh to Twelfth streets ... presenting a surface of yellow or white clay, cut into by deep gullies, and without trees except one or two scraggy and dying sycamores. The streets named were mud roads, along which an omnibus scrambled once a day, to the steamboat wharf, and foot travel paced its muddy or dusty way over the bleak, unhospitable common in zig-zag meanderings.[11]

In 1822, Congress allowed the city to separate four blocks from the Mall and divide them into lots for sale to the public (see page 62). Ten years later, Congress granted the city nearly half of what was left of the park. Two new streets, A Street North and A Street South, would be laid out along the length of the Mall. A narrow strip of parkland between these two streets would remain, but the rest of the Mall would be sold.

Congress reversed itself the following year, recognizing the value of the park to the city in the future, when the population density would increase. At the same time, it appropriated a modest sum for the commissioner of public buildings to plant grass, lay out paths, and enclose the Mall with a fence, presumably to protect it from stray animals. The funds were not enough to have much effect, however, and 15 years passed before Congress made another appropriation for the improvement of the Mall.[12]

This sketch by Seth Eastman depicts the Mall as it appeared in 1851. In the foreground is the mouth of the Washington Canal, now the site of Constitution Avenue. On the far bank of the canal is the Jefferson Stone, a short stone column that was installed in 1804 as part of Thomas Jefferson's attempt to establish a national prime meridian in Washington (see page 94). Beyond it is the Washington Monument, begun in 1848.

Andrew Jackson Downing (1815–1852) was America's first prominent landscape architect. In 1851, he completed a landscape plan for the Mall. However, work on the project stalled the following year, after Downing drowned in a steamship accident on the Hudson River.

This print, *Washington, D.C., with Projected Improvements*, by Benjamin Franklin Smith Jr., was published in 1852. It shows the Mall as it would have appeared if Andrew Jackson Downing's landscaping plan had been implemented. The Washington Monument, which was still under construction in 1852, is shown completed. The original plans for the monument, by architect Robert Mills, included a 100-foot-high pantheon, which was never built.

IN 1847, the board of regents of the newly formed Smithsonian Institution laid the cornerstone of their new headquarters, a picturesque red sandstone building now known as the Castle. It was the beginning of a flurry of activity on the Mall, for work soon began on the Botanic Garden, the Washington Monument, and an overall landscaping scheme. The Mall at this time was the domain of the commissioner of public buildings, who had a wide variety of responsibilities, including selling lots in the city; maintaining the President's House; and caring for, and policing, the public parks in the capital. The commissioner's office was established in 1816 and was, administratively, a direct descendant of the three commissioners who oversaw the District in its earliest days. (Responsibility for the Mall would pass to the Army Corps of Engineers in 1867 and then to the National Park Service in 1933.)

On July 4, 1848, an elaborate public ceremony marked the setting of the cornerstone of the Washington Monument. A private association undertook this important project with the best of intentions, but it soon ran out of funds, and the monument sat as an unfinished stump for more than 20 years (see pages 90–93).

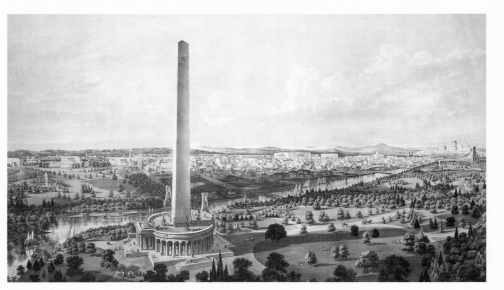

In October 1850, a group of influential Washingtonians contacted Andrew Jackson Downing of New York, inviting him to design a landscaping plan for the Mall. Downing was the most prominent landscape architect in America, having written three important books on the subject, and was an expert on horticulture as well. Downing came to Washington in November 1850 and thoroughly inspected the Mall. He completed his plan that winter, and in April 1851, it was approved by President Millard Fillmore. Downing's naturalistic landscaping style was characterized by winding paths, scattered trees, and irregularly shaped pools that emulated, and improved upon, nature. It was the antithesis of the classical landscaping that inspired L'Enfant, which was marked by geometry, symmetry, and order.

Downing was an early advocate of large urban parks—there were only a few in the country at that time—and he was a strong believer in their civilizing properties. Besides being a fine place for public recreation, his Mall would have been educational, with many varieties of trees and other plants suited to Washington's climate, all well labeled. The President's Park was included in his plan as well, and a suspension bridge crossing the canal would have connected the park to the Mall.

Work soon began under Downing's supervision, with funds appropriated by Congress. Tragically, Downing died the following year, on July 28, 1852, while trying to save fellow passengers after the steamship *Henry Clay* caught fire on the Hudson River. He was only 36 years old. Work continued under the supervision of others, but without his enthusiasm, the project soon withered. Only a portion of the Smithsonian grounds, between Seventh and Twelfth streets north of the Castle, was completed.

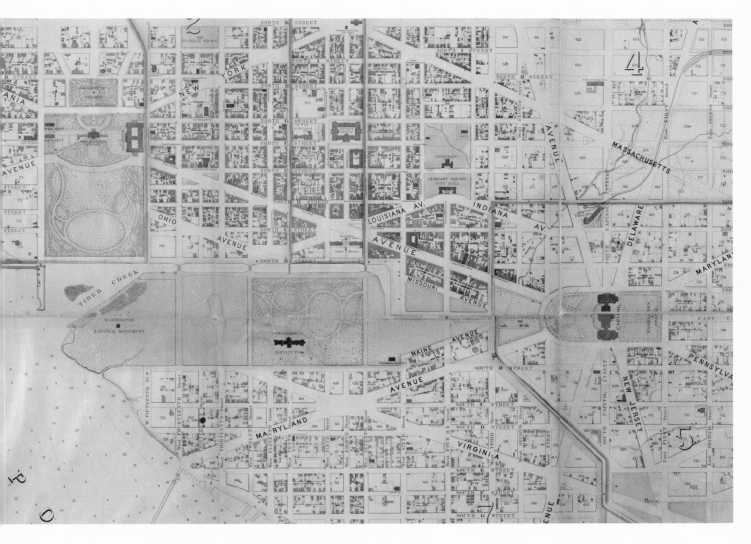

This map, published in 1857 by Albert Boschke, is said to be the most accurate ever made of the city, since every building was individually measured. Shown here is a detail; the complete map covers Washington south of Florida Avenue. Boschke, an immigrant from Germany, worked for the U.S. Coast Survey in Washington and produced this map for his own account. In 1861, after he published a second map showing the entire District of Columbia, the federal government confiscated the plates to prevent it from falling into Confederate hands. The one shown here has a number of interesting features. On the far left is the Seventeenth Street wharf and an extension of the Chesapeake and Ohio Canal. Facing the Mall are Missouri and Maine avenues, which were closed in the 1930s. On the right, the grounds of the Capitol appear before they were extended to the north and south.

As the Civil War approached, the development of the Mall was understandably forgotten by Congress. It was not until the 1870s that work would resume, this time carried out by the Army Corps of Engineers. The engineers in charge, Nathaniel Michler and his successor, Orville Babcock, considered their work the completion of Downing's scheme. Michler and Babcock followed Downing's plan in spirit, but not in detail. Their Victorian landscaping was also a radical departure from the intentions of L'Enfant, as it ignored the axial relationships that were so important to him and blocked his vistas with trees.

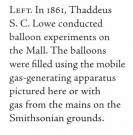

government with various scientific investigations related to the war effort, and it prosecuted its normal scientific activities as best it could, it spite of wartime difficulties.

Thaddeus S. C. Lowe, a pioneer balloonist, conducted experiments on the grounds of the armory in 1861, the first year of the Civil War. With the support of Joseph Henry, Secretary of War Simon Cameron, and President Abraham Lincoln, Lowe hoped to demonstrate the balloon's utility for military reconnaissance. On June 18, 1861, Lowe raised his balloon above the Mall to a height said to have been 500 feet. Over a telegraph wire connected to the White House, Lowe issued a brief message to the president that noted the broad view of the city and described the dispatch as "the first . . . ever telegraphed from an aerial station."[13] Lowe soon established a balloon corps for the Union army and successfully performed aerial reconnaissance of Confederate positions.

IN THE 1850s, the War Department constructed an armory for the militia of the District of Columbia (see pages 82–84) on the site now occupied by the National Air and Space Museum. During the Civil War, the armory became a hospital, and dozens of wooden buildings, including wards for wounded soldiers and a chapel, were constructed in the square surrounding it, extending halfway across the Mall. Known as Armory Square Hospital, it was said to receive the most grievously wounded, since it was the closest of dozens of Washington hospitals to the wharves at the foot of Seventh Street. The Capitol also served as both a hospital and a barracks for troops at the start of the war. The U.S. Army Commissary Corps used the grounds of the Washington Monument as a depot for cattle, which fed the troops stationed in and around the city.

Joseph Henry, secretary of the Smithsonian Institution, was assiduously neutral during the war. Perhaps as an expression of the neutrality of science, the Smithsonian did not fly the American flag during those years. Nevertheless, the institution assisted the federal

The Washington Monument remained an unfinished stump for more than 20 years. In the foreground of this c. 1870 photograph is the mouth of the old Washington Canal.

UNTIL 1867, the Mall was the responsibility of the commissioner of public buildings. Congress fired the last commissioner, Benjamin Brown French, for his support of President Andrew Johnson. The Radical Republicans, who despised Johnson for his policy of leniency toward the defeated South after the Civil War, got hold of a poem that French had written in praise of Johnson and mockingly read it before the House of Representatives. As punishment, they abolished his position, and his duties relating to the Capitol passed to the Architect of the Capitol.[14]

French's responsibility for the White House, the Mall, and the other parks in the city went to the U.S. Army Corps of Engineers. To perform the job, the army created the Office of Public Buildings and Grounds and appointed Major Nathaniel Michler as the first officer in charge. Over the next few years, Michler urged Congress to complete the Washington Monument, develop the Mall as a park with a unified landscaping scheme, and either improve or fill the canal, but Congress appropriated only enough funds for the most basic maintenance.

In 1870 the condition of the various squares that made up the Mall varied greatly. Work on the Washington Monument had stopped 16 years earlier, and it was now a 156-foot-tall unfinished stump. The landfill operations that would create Potomac Park had not yet begun, and the waters of the Potomac still reached almost to the base of the monument. At the foot of Seventeenth Street there was a wharf that extended south into the river from B Street. It dated from the earliest years of the capital and was still in use by small craft. Beyond the wharf were mud flats, about 1,000 acres in extent and covered with eel grass. Nearby, the old canal emptied into the Potomac. It was little more than an open sewer, and filth slowly made its way down to the river, where it lodged in the flats and baked in the summer sun.

To the southeast of the monument was the ornate brick headquarters of the Department of Agriculture, completed in 1868. On the south side of the Agriculture grounds there was a formal garden, while on the north side, an arboretum was under construction. The Smithsonian grounds, a 50-acre square between Seventh and Twelfth streets, were in a similar state. The portion north of the Castle, the Smithsonian's only building at the time, had been finished by Andrew Jackson Downing in a naturalistic manner, while the southern portion was an open lawn. A picket fence enclosed the entire square.

Between Sixth and Seventh streets was Armory Square, but the armory itself was unoccupied, and the wooden buildings built during the Civil War for the hospital had been demolished. Between Third and Sixth streets, the canal ran along the center of the Mall. On the north side of the canal, the Agriculture Department and the Engineer Corps maintained separate propagating gardens. The south side was occasionally used by visiting circuses, but otherwise it was vacant. At the eastern end of the Mall, the Botanic Garden conservatory was still unfinished, and the grounds were barren.[15]

The poor condition of the Mall reflected the sorry state of the city as a whole. Few of the streets were properly graded or paved, and the sewer system was rudimentary. In 1870 a powerful movement was afoot to move the capital to some distant city, perhaps Saint Louis, supported by congressmen and business interests from the Midwest. President Ulysses S. Grant opposed the move and implied that he would veto any bill that would relocate the federal government. Grant strongly supported improvements to the city as a way of reinforcing its role as the national capital, and he encouraged Congress to appropriate money to that end. America was

This photograph, c. 1879, captures a view of the Mall looking east from the Smithsonian Institution. In the center are rail cars on sidings belonging to the Baltimore and Potomac Railroad Station, which was located just outside the frame to the left. The station and tracks, which nearly cut the Mall in two, were the first target of the 1902 McMillan Commission. On the right is the round gas storage tank of the Washington Gas Light Company, located on the site of the present-day National Museum of the American Indian. Near the gas tank was a notorious slum (see page 62). An adjoining portion of the Mall, located between Third and Four and One-Half streets, was described by the *Washington Post* in 1897 as "perhaps the foulest park in the entire city" and "the abiding place of loafers, thugs, thieves, and dissolute men and women." The newspaper blamed the problem on the undergrowth, which by that time had grown quite dense. In the foreground are the grounds of the Smithsonian Institution, begun by Andrew Jackson Downing in 1851.

expanding rapidly, and the president believed that the city should be worthy of the pride of every American. Finally, as a Republican during Reconstruction, he expected that a world-class capital city would symbolically emphasize the federal government's superior relationship to the states.[16]

In 1871, Grant supported the establishment of a territorial government for the city, with a governor as its chief executive. Alexander "Boss" Shepherd, initially the controlling member of the city's Board of Public Works and later governor, immediately undertook a vast program of civic improvement. Shepherd spent the city into bankruptcy in a frenzied effort to transform Washington into an attractive and modern city equal to any in the world. He graded and paved the streets, laid sidewalks, installed sewers and gas lights, planted trees by the thousands, and filled in the pestiferous Washington Canal.

At the same time, Congress finally appropriated a substantial sum for the improvement of the Mall. After seven decades of ignoring the public grounds at its doorstep, it was at long last paying to see the Mall transformed into a finished park. Major Orville E. Babcock, who had replaced Michler as officer in charge of public buildings and grounds, began the work in 1871. Since his office had only a few employees, he acted as a contractor and hired laborers to perform the work. Babcock filled and graded the grounds and installed drains. He planted trees, shrubs, and grass; laid out carriage paths and walks; and installed fences and gas lights. The Botanic Garden and the Agriculture grounds received a similar treatment, although they were not within his domain (these portions of the Mall were maintained by the Architect of the Capitol and the Department of Agriculture, respectively).

The northern and western sides of the Washington Monument grounds were low and wet, and to avoid the extensive filling that would have been necessary, Babcock constructed several ponds there. The U.S. Fish Commission soon began using them for raising fish, and one of the ponds was later used for several years by the city government as a public swimming basin. The last of the ponds was filled in in 1911.[17]

In 1873, the city's Board of Public Works installed a tall iron fence and decorative stone posts along the northern edge of the Mall between Seventh and Fifteenth streets. The fence (see page 79), which came from the grounds of the Capitol and Judiciary Square, was probably intended to separate the Mall from what would become the Federal Triangle, which at that time was a notorious slum and red-light district.

In 1875, Orville Babcock wrote that the Smithsonian grounds were very popular with the public, who came to view the curiosities in the museum and take advantage of the shade of the magnificent trees. However, he wrote, "These grounds have been avoided by the better class of people after night-fall on account of the number of disreputable characters of both sexes who assembled here." Two night watchmen were unable to control the problem, so Babcock installed gas lights on all of the paths, and this apparently helped.[18] To contain insect pests, Babcock imported hundreds of English and German sparrows and provided them with houses in the park.

Babcock's work was essentially complete by 1876. The Mall was now a continuous park, well finished with trees, paths, lamps, and benches.[19] It would remain to Babcock's successor, Lieutenant Colonel Thomas Lincoln Casey, to complete the Washington Monument, which had been abandoned more than 20 years earlier.

Daniel Burnham (1846–1912) "never hurried and never rested," wrote Charles Moore; his "mind worked on a grand scale; he saw things in the large." Burnham was chief designer of the 1893 Chicago world's fair and sketched the broad outlines of the 1902 McMillan Plan for Washington.

RIGHT. The World's Columbian Exposition, held in Chicago in 1893, had a profound influence on American architecture. The façades were made of staff, a mixture of cement, plaster, and jute (a plant fiber) that resembled marble. The buildings were destroyed shortly after the fair.

IN 1888, as the Washington Monument opened to the public, the Army Corps of Engineers was busy filling the mud flats along the banks of the Potomac. The work, intended to clear the channel for navigation and eliminate the noxious flats, would ultimately add 628 acres of new land to the city. Washington was competing to hold the World's Columbian Exposition, a fair commemorating the 400th anniversary of the discovery of America by Columbus, and the new land was proposed as the site of the fair. Washington lost its bid to Chicago, but the exposition nevertheless had a profound effect on the architecture of the capital city and the development of the Mall.

Held in Chicago in 1893, the Columbian Exposition had hundreds of temporary exhibition buildings in a park that covered more than 600 acres. The centerpiece was the Court of Honor, a broad canal surrounded by an extraordinary array of buildings. Elaborate but ephemeral, they recalled the grandeur of ancient civilizations but were built to last only a few months. The building's façades were made of plaster resembling marble, and they reflected brilliantly in the sun and water. The effect on visitors, who numbered more than 20 million, was electrifying. The Court of Honor became a vision for what American cities ought to be.

Daniel H. Burnham, a prominent Chicago architect, was the exposition's chief designer, and his preference for Beaux-Arts architecture had a deciding effect on the fair. To design the buildings around the Court of Honor, he assembled a group of the most important and fashionable East Coast architectural firms, all of whom favored that style. Charles F. McKim, who was responsible for the Agriculture building at the fair, was one of the leading proponents of Beaux-Arts in America. Burnham and McKim would later play a decisive role in shaping the National Mall in Washington as authors of the 1902 McMillan Plan. Beaux-Arts architecture would come to dominate the capital city, as it had the Chicago fair.

Beaux-Arts architecture takes its name from the French national school of art, the Ecole des Beaux-Arts in Paris. Many prominent American architects of the late nineteenth and early twentieth centuries were trained there, including Richard Morris Hunt, Charles McKim, and John Russell Pope. At the Ecole, students learned principles of design and a methodology for planning buildings, focusing on monumental structures such as libraries, museums, and railroad stations. As an architectural term, Beaux-Arts refers in its narrowest sense to the architecture taught at the Ecole from roughly 1850 to 1914. Beaux-Arts was not so much a new style, as a method for combining ancient, Renaissance, and Baroque elements into imaginative new compositions.

The Ecole taught that the purpose of a building should be reflected in both its overall design and its decoration, so Beaux-Arts buildings frequently have decorative sculpture, murals, and inscriptions that reflect the building's purpose. Columns, pilasters, grand staircases, and monumental arches are common features as well. Symmetry is important, and the principal components of these buildings are normally arranged along axes that intersect at right angles. A typical Beaux-Arts building is clad in white or light gray stone, but its structure is modern, with a steel frame. Examples on the Mall include the Natural History museum and the Freer Gallery of Art. The Lincoln Memorial, the Jefferson Memorial, and the West Building of the National Gallery of Art are Beaux-Arts as well, although they are more purely classical in style.

No ASPECT of Washington history has been more closely examined by historians than the 1902 Senate Park Commission Plan, better known today as the McMillan Plan. Sponsored by the U.S. Senate and drawn up by a commission of four prominent architects and artists, the plan was a wildly ambitious scheme for the redevelopment of Washington's park system and monumental core. Some of the city's most important icons, including the Lincoln Memorial and the reflecting pool, first appeared as part of the plan.

The McMillan Commission hoped to return the Mall to the intentions of its original designer, Peter Charles L'Enfant. The Victorian landscaping of the Mall, which blocked L'Enfant's vistas with trees and buildings, would be swept aside and replaced with a broad greensward flanked by symmetric rows of elm trees and white monumental buildings. Everything would be formal and geometric, in contrast to the naturalistic and picturesque landscaping of Downing's scheme for the Mall.

Commensurate with America's vast expansion since L'Enfant's time, the commission proposed expanding the city's monumental core to fill a kite-shaped region bounded by Pennsylvania, Maryland, and New York avenues. The 628 acres of new land to the west of the Washington Monument would accommodate a mile-long extension of the Mall, terminated by a monument to Lincoln on the banks of the Potomac River. Following Beaux-Arts principles, the buildings in the core area would be white, monumental, uniform in height, and arranged in orderly ranks. Existing buildings that conformed with the plan, such as the Corcoran Gallery of Art, could remain, but the others would be demolished. The McMillan Plan provided much-needed guidelines for the location of future federal buildings, and it offered an official architectural style for the city.

The McMillan Commission was created largely at the instigation of Glenn Brown, secretary of the American Institute of Architects (AIA) in Washington. As an architect, he is probably best known for the "Buffalo Bridge," which carries Q Street over Rock Creek. He was an advocate of quality architecture in Washington and lobbied for a greater role for private architects in federal projects.

Brown brought the AIA's annual meeting to Washington in 1900, the centennial of the establishment of the federal government there.

The theme of the meeting was the unified beautification of the capital, and Brown ensured that the most capable architects in the country presented plans. Among them was landscape architect Frederick Law Olmsted Jr., who called for returning the Mall to the intentions of L'Enfant. (Many of his suggestions later found their way into the McMillan Plan.) To bring the ideas presented at the conference to the attention of Congress, the AIA formed a legislative committee, which soon met with Senator James McMillan, a Republican from Michigan and chairman of the Senate Committee on the District of Columbia. McMillan was receptive, since he was

Looking west from the Washington Monument toward the site of the Lincoln Memorial in 1899. The newly created land was officially Potomac Park, but it was still covered with weeds and brush. The 1902 McMillan Plan included a bold proposal for the completion of the park.

a firm believer in large-scale city planning and was keenly interested in developing a master plan for Washington. He had played a large role in building a park system for Detroit and had recently sponsored a plan for the improvement of the Mall, a scheme by landscape architect Samuel Parsons Jr. that was poorly received by critics.

After meeting with the AIA, McMillan introduced (on March 8, 1901) a Senate Resolution authorizing his District committee to make "plans for the development and improvement of the entire park system of the District of Columbia" using "the services of such experts as may be necessary." Expenses would be paid out of Senate contingency funds. This arrangement allowed him to bypass committees in the House, but it caused problems later with representatives who were offended that they had not been consulted in the preparation of the plans. Joseph Cannon, a powerful Republican representative from Illinois, would prove to be a vociferous opponent.

Development of the plans proceeded rapidly. In consultation with the AIA, McMillan appointed Daniel H. Burnham and Frederick Law Olmsted Jr. to a commission that would develop the plans for Washington. It would be known as the Senate Park Commission or, in later years, the McMillan Commission, after the senator. Authorized to bring in a third member, Burnham appointed architect Charles Follen McKim.

Daniel H. Burnham, the great impresario of the Chicago fair, was the chairman of the commission. Burnham was one of the most prominent architects in the country and a strong advocate of comprehensive city planning. As a partner in the Chicago architectural firm Burnham and Root, he played an important role in the development of the steel-framed office building. Burnham was a brilliant and energetic administrator and organizer. Always a big thinker, his motto was "Make no little plans, for they have no magic to stir men's blood. Make big plans." His exact words, or whether he said them at all, are a matter of debate, but they capture his thinking precisely. Burnham expanded the scope of the commission's work, arguing that it was their duty to develop the best possible plans, regardless of the cost.

Charles McKim, of New York, was the creative genius behind McKim, Mead and White, the most successful American architectural firm of the late nineteenth century. His Boston Public Library was perhaps the archetypal Beaux-Arts building in America. McKim saw Beaux-Arts not as the imitation of historic styles, as some did, but as a timeless, universal architecture. He was scholarly, reserved, and, in his work, a perfectionist.

Each of the men had a connection to the Chicago fair. Besides serving as Burnham's right-hand man at the exposition, McKim designed the Agriculture building on the Court of Honor. The third member of the commission, Frederick Law Olmsted Jr., was the son of Frederick Law Olmsted Sr., who developed the fair's overall landscaping plan. The elder Olmsted, who was acknowledged as the greatest American landscape architect of the nineteenth century, designed Central Park in New York and the grounds of the U.S. Capitol. The younger Olmsted, who had a practice in Brookline, Massachusetts, was a highly respected and accomplished landscape architect in his own right.

Burnham and McKim soon invited sculptor Augustus Saint-Gaudens to join the group. The two architects had worked with him on the Chicago fair, where he had been the chief advisor on sculpture, and they valued his judgment. Besides, Saint-Gaudens was widely recognized as the foremost American sculptor of his age, and his prestigious name would add weight to their plans in the eyes of Congress and the public. Saint-Gaudens and McKim were good friends; he had designed sculpture for McKim's Agriculture building at the Chicago fair and for the Boston Public Library. On the Washington work, the others consulted him often, but the sculptor's poor health prevented him from taking a more active role.

McMillan's personal secretary, Charles Moore, served as secretary to the commission. A political insider and a powerful facilitator, Moore would play a large role in ensuring that the plan would be implemented. Well informed on matters of art, he had once worked as a journalist and was a skilled writer. Moore was editor of the commission's report to the Senate, and he later wrote articles for national magazines explaining the plan to the public.

In June 1901, Burnham, McKim, Olmsted, and Moore left for a grand tour of Europe. They visited many of the great civic spaces and urban parks in Paris, Rome, Venice, Vienna, Budapest, and London. In France, they looked for inspiration in the gardens of Fontainebleau, Versailles, and Vaux-le-Vicomte, all designed by the great seventeenth-century French landscape architect André Le Nôtre, who no doubt had a deep influence on L'Enfant. At Vaux-le-Vicomte, a cart "carried them along the broad driveways, and they pictured what the Washington Mall would be when L'Enfant's design had been restored."[20] In Rome, whose hot climate reminded them of Washington, they decided that water fountains were appropriate for the capital city. At that time, Budapest was considered the

Paris of Central Europe. On one side of the Danube was historic Buda, and on the other side was Pest, which Charles Moore described as the most modern city in the world. In England, they visited parks such as those at Hatfield House and Hampton Court.

The last stop of their tour was London. While there, Burnham met with Alexander Cassatt, president of the Pennsylvania Railroad. Burnham had been hired to design a replacement for the Pennsylvania's small and decrepit depot on the Mall (see pages 80–81). He had tried to convince the railroad to build on a new site south of the Mall, but was told that his job was to design the station, not select its location. Burnham knew that the owners of the Pennsylvania Railroad had a lot of clout in Congress and could not

OPPOSITE (top to bottom):

Glenn Brown (1854–1932), secretary of the American Institute of Architects, lobbied persistently for the improvement of the city and was an important force behind the creation of the McMillan Commission.

Senator James McMillan (1838–1902), a Republican from Michigan, sponsored the 1902 Senate Park Commission Plan for Washington, later known as the McMillan Plan.

Frederick Law Olmsted Jr. (1870–1957), a renowned landscape architect, was still a young man when he served on the McMillan Commission in 1901–1902.

Charles F. McKim (1847–1909), one of the nation's most prominent architects, did most of the work on the McMillan Plan. His influence on the Mall was second only to L'Enfant's.

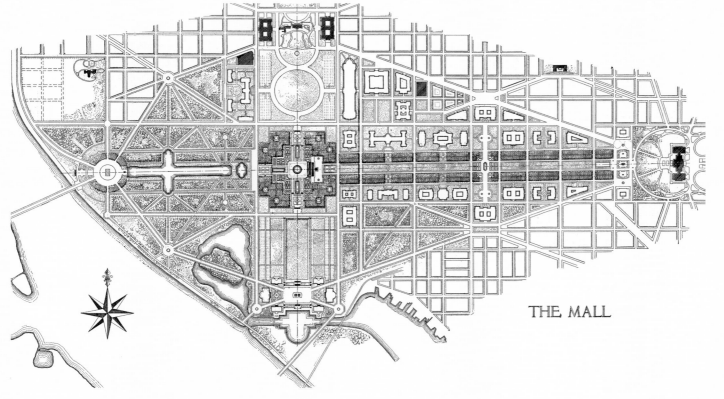

THE MALL

LEFT. In its 1902 plan, the McMillan Commission tilted the main axis of the Mall to the southwest to compensate for the location of the Washington Monument, an effect that is visible here and on present-day maps of the city. The plan would have radically reshaped the Tidal Basin, an idea that was later dropped.

The 1902 McMillan Plan proposed expanding the monumental core of Washington outward to fill a vast kite-shaped area. This rendering, made for an exhibit that accompanied the public debut of the plan, shows the Lincoln Memorial and the reflecting pool for the first time, decades before they were actually built.

be forced to give up the choice site on the Mall. If the station, with its tracks, train sheds, and steam locomotives, were allowed to remain there, his plans for the improvement of the park would never come to fruition.

Burnham hoped to bring Cassatt to Paris to share with him the commission's vision for the Mall. Revealing the influence that Paris had on their work, Charles Moore wrote:

The Commission had determined to ask Mr. Cassatt to go back to Paris with them, and, standing on the terrace overlooking the Place de la Concorde, to take note of the glories of a city designed as a work of art—the Palace of the Tuileries as the Capitol, the Tuileries Gardens as the Mall, the Obelisk in the crossing of two Paris axes as the Washington Monument centers the Capitol and White House axes; and then a Lincoln Memorial as a national monument in location at the termination of the composition, and also as a center of distribution comparable to the Arc de Triomphe de l'Etoile.[21]

The trip to Paris was unnecessary, however. At their brief meeting, Cassatt told Burnham that the Pennsylvania Railroad had recently merged with the Baltimore and Ohio, which had its own station on New Jersey Avenue, N.W. Since the combined enterprise did not need two depots in Washington, he would be willing to abandon the Mall site and build a new station north of the Capitol if Congress would bear some of the costs. A jubilant Burnham reported the news to McMillan, who won approval of the plan in Congress. Union Station (so named because it unified two lines) opened in 1907, and the old station on the Mall was demolished the following year.

After they returned to the United States, Burnham was occupied with Union Station and devoted relatively little time to the Park Commission. His role was to oversee the project, and he developed the broad outlines of the plan. McKim did most of the work; he finalized the plans at his office in New York, working out the details and refining and expanding on Burnham's ideas. Frederick Law Olmsted Jr. was charged with planning the outlying parks in the District of Columbia and the connections between them. Throughout the fall of 1901, the four consulted constantly with one another as the project progressed.

Each of the men served without pay, simply for the opportunity to work on such an important project. McKim, one of the most successful architects in the country, set aside his practice for the better part of a year to work almost exclusively on the McMillan Plan. He believed that it was a matter of national importance. Early on, the commission met with President William McKinley and received his approval. They were confident that they had powerful friends who could ensure that their carefully conceived plans would be carried out.

On September 6, 1901, President McKinley was shot by an assassin in Buffalo, New York, and died a week later. Theodore Roosevelt, only 42 years old and possessed of boundless energy, assumed the presidency. Roosevelt and his successor, William Howard Taft, became strong supporters of the commission's work. They no doubt saw the McMillan Plan as a reflection of their Progressive ideals. Just as Roosevelt reformed business by breaking up the trusts, the McMillan Plan would reform Washington by replacing the chaotic Victorian Mall, and the dingy commercial buildings that surrounded it, with rows of white marble buildings and a beautiful formal park.

McMillan presented the plan to the Senate on January 15, 1902. That afternoon, an exhibit illustrating and promoting the plan opened at the Corcoran Gallery of Art. With Charles Moore and Senator McMillan acting as guides, President Roosevelt and members of his cabinet toured the exhibit. There were two large models of the city, each about 17 feet long. The first was an extremely detailed and accurate rendition of central Washington as it existed in 1901. The second was the city as it would appear if the McMillan Plan were carried out. They were mounted at eye level and dramatically lit, and visitors could have a bird's-eye view from a raised platform. The walls were lined with large, beautiful paintings of the future Mall. The president was enthusiastic.

Curiously, there is only one extant photograph of the exhibit, which shows workers applying finishing touches to the models before the exhibit opened. Portions of the models are currently on display at the National Building Museum, 401 F Street, N.W., in Washington. Only a few of the original paintings have survived and are hanging in the offices of the Commission of Fine Arts.

This is the only known photograph of the 1902 exhibit at the Corcoran Gallery of Art that introduced the McMillan Plan to the public. The exhibit included detailed models of present and future Washington, seen here under preparation.

By 1900, the Mall was a finished park, albeit one very different from today. It was densely planted with trees and lined with ornate brick buildings, and visitors could stroll along winding gravel paths beneath a canopy of branches. Tourists could visit the Botanic Garden, the Army Medical Museum, the Smithsonian Institution, the Agriculture Museum, the Washington Monument, and other attractions.

THE MOST DRAMATIC aspect of the new plan was the extension of the Mall westward, almost one mile across the new landfill to the Potomac. On the banks of the river, in perfect alignment with the Washington Monument and the Capitol, would be a memorial to Abraham Lincoln. It was the most important new site on the Mall, and the commission believed that it should be reserved for the 16th president, who was "the one man in our history as a nation who is worthy to be named with George Washington."[22]

The location of the Washington Monument, however, presented the commission with a dilemma. According to the L'Enfant Plan, the monument should have been located directly west of the Capitol and south of the White House. Instead, it was built somewhat to the southeast of the proper site, presumably because of poor soil conditions. Now, the entire main axis of the Mall would have to be tilted to the southwest to compensate. The commission considered moving the obelisk, but dismissed the idea as too expensive. Today, the tilted axis is readily apparent when viewing a map, but it is not perceptible on the ground.

To emphasize the Mall's main axis, the commission proposed a broad lawn, 300 feet wide, stretching from the Capitol to the Washington Monument. Flanking this greensward would be four rows of elm trees and long parallel carriage drives. Behind the elms would be rows of museums and buildings devoted to science. Gone would be the dense Victorian plantings, and the Mall would be restored to the intentions of L'Enfant. The commission pointed out that this treatment could be found in many parks in Europe and the United States.

The Lincoln Memorial, as proposed by the McMillan Commission, had an open array of columns similar to the Brandenburg Gate in Berlin. In front of the memorial, standing in the open air, would be a bronze statue of Lincoln (see the rendering on page 104). The commission placed the memorial at the center of a *rond point*, or traffic circle. Their inspiration was the Arc de Triomphe in Paris, which stands in L'Étoile, a large *rond point* at the head of the Champs-Élysées. Unfortunately, the commission failed to anticipate the popularity of the automobile (there were only a handful in Washington in 1902). Today, the eastern half of the *rond point* is a pedestrian plaza, while the western half is a busy highway.

Between the Lincoln Memorial and the Washington Monument, the commission placed a long cruciform reflecting pool.

They suggested that it be similar to pools at Versailles and Fontainebleau in France, and Hampton Court in England, which they had seen on their European tour. The pool was completed in the early 1920s, but the transverse arms were never built, since the site of the northern arm was blocked by a temporary government office building. Moreover, it was felt that the arms would impede circulation on the Mall.

By the time that the commission began its work, plans for a Memorial Bridge between Washington and Arlington Cemetery had already been under consideration for a number of years. In 1899, Congress sponsored a design competition for a span that would have been located roughly on the site of today's Roosevelt Bridge. The winning design was presented to Congress in 1900, but

This recent photograph dramatically illustrates the changes wrought by the McMillan Commission, which in 1902 proposed replacing the dense Victorian plantings with a central greensward flanked by parallel drives, rows of elms, and white classical buildings. The landscaping work was completed by the National Park Service in the 1930s, and the results can be seen today.

no funds were appropriated for its construction. The McMillan Commission proposed adapting this design to a new location between the *rond point* and Arlington Cemetery and suggested omitting two large towers from the center of the span because they would have competed with the Lincoln Memorial. Eventually, this design was dropped entirely, and when work began on the bridge in 1926, it was following an entirely new set of plans.

The McMillan Commission devoted considerable attention to the Mall's cross axis, an imaginary line that connects the White House with the site of the Jefferson Memorial. Although it was an important part of the L'Enfant Plan, this secondary axis had been ignored when the Mall was improved in the nineteenth century. To restore and emphasize it, the commission proposed a pantheon honoring American heroes, or a memorial to an unspecified person, on the Tidal Basin directly south of the White House. Surrounding this monument would be buildings providing a wide variety of recreational facilities to the people of Washington, including a stadium, a gymnasium, and playgrounds. Although it would have been used for informal purposes, "Washington Common," as the commission suggested calling it, was intensely formal, with neoclassical buildings arranged symmetrically around the central pantheon. The Tidal Basin would have been radically reshaped into several smaller basins, with facilities for swimming and boating. Ultimately, the proposed monument was realized as the Jefferson Memorial, but the Tidal Basin was left intact to lower costs and preserve the beloved cherry trees. Recreational facilities were constructed nearby, in East Potomac Park.

For the Washington Monument grounds, the commission proposed a formal garden to the west of the monument, which would be reached by a 300-foot-wide marble staircase. In the garden, elm trees, terraces, fountains, and sculpture were arranged around a central pool, all calculated to emphasize the Mall's two axes. Since the garden was 40 feet below the base of the monument, it would require removing a large part of the hill supporting the shaft. This large cut would clear the vista from the White House to the proposed monument on the Tidal Basin, further emphasizing the cross

By the turn of the twentieth century, the plantings on the Mall had become quite dense. This photograph shows the view north from the entrance porch of the Smithsonian Castle.

axis. The commission described the garden as the "gem of the Mall system," and no part of the plan absorbed more of their attention. Unfortunately, engineering studies undertaken in 1930 showed that the deep excavations could have had a catastrophic effect on the stability of the monument, so the plans for the garden were set aside.

Congress had not officially accepted the McMillan Plan, and Senator McMillan's death in August 1902 dealt it a serious blow. McMillan knew the plan better than anyone in Congress, and he had been its staunchest supporter. Whether it would be followed or ignored was yet to be determined.

THE McMILLAN COMMISSION ceased to exist after it presented its plan on January 15, 1902, but the former members of the commission, along with Charles Moore, continued to defend the plan in an unofficial capacity. Charles McKim was involved that year with renovations to the White House, and he knew President Theodore Roosevelt well. Roosevelt, William H. Taft, and Elihu Root supported the commission's recommendations, and they were powerful allies. Root, as secretary of war, oversaw the Army Corps of Engineers, which was responsible for the maintenance and improvement of the Mall. The McMillan Commission had consulted with him frequently as they developed their plans to ensure his support.

Since the McMillan Plan did not carry the force of law, it was crucial that it be respected from the beginning, or it was likely to be ignored forever after. Its first important test concerned the location of the new Agriculture Department building. The McMillan Commission had determined that there should be at least 445 feet between the façades of the buildings along the Mall and the centerline. Since the Mall's main axis was tilted to the southwest to accommodate the Washington Monument, the land available to the Agriculture Department on the south side of the Mall was severely limited. Reasoning that it would be only a minor modification to the plan, President Roosevelt gave Secretary of Agriculture James Wilson permission to build out to a line only 300 feet from the center. When Charles McKim heard of this, he went to Roosevelt. The president said that if McKim could get the Senate to support the 445-foot setback, then he would reconsider.

Senator Francis Newlands of Nevada, a man friendly to the cause, persuaded Jacob Gallinger, the new chairman of the Senate Committee on the District of Columbia, to hold a hearing on the matter. (Newlands is best known in Washington as the developer of the Chevy Chase subdivision.) At the hearing, held on March 12, 1904, Burnham and McKim argued persuasively for the 445-foot setback, detailing their long deliberations over this part of the plan. Modifying the setback would require narrowing the greensward, which had to be at least 300 feet wide; it could be wider, but not an

inch narrower. Gallinger was impressed by their arguments and agreed to support their position. Roosevelt promptly reversed himself and asked Secretary Wilson to respect the 445-foot setback.

As the Agriculture Department started the excavations, McKim saw that the new building would be located off center, in line with Thirteenth Street, like the old headquarters, rather than centered between Twelfth and Fourteenth streets. At the same time, McKim found that the base of the new structure would be too high—the Mall was supposed to rise gradually to the Washington Monument, and the effect would be spoiled. McKim appealed to Roosevelt through Secretary of War Taft, and in a meeting at the White House, Roosevelt decided the matter in McKim's favor.

During the remainder of the decade, the federal government erected several buildings in Washington's monumental core, and each followed the McMillan Plan, in both style and location. In 1904, work began on the new National Museum, now the National Museum of Natural History. It was the first building to respect the new alignment of the Mall's main axis: The façade was angled slightly to the southwest to squarely face the long greensward. The museum building, clad in white granite, followed the Beaux-Arts principles favored by the commission. The Russell Senate and Cannon House office buildings, completed in 1908 facing the grounds of the Capitol, conformed to the plan as well.

As the McMillan Commission was working on its scheme for Washington, planning for a memorial to Ulysses S. Grant was already underway. The commission created a site for the memorial on the Mall in a broad plaza just west of First Street. The plaza would be called Union Square after its central location and the Civil War heroes who would be honored there.

The Grant Memorial Commission, which had been authorized by Congress to select a site and a sculptor, favored a location on the Ellipse, south of the White House. The jury appointed to choose the sculptor, however, suggested that the memorial be built on the site specified in the McMillan Plan. Their preference should not be surprising, since the jurors included Daniel Burnham, Charles McKim, and Augustus Saint-Gaudens. Congress accepted their

The McMillan Commission, in its 1902 plan for Washington's parks, described a gem at the center of the Mall: a formal garden that would provide a majestic setting for the Washington Monument and emphasize the axial relationships among the Capitol, the White House, and the most important monuments. However, engineering studies conducted in 1930 determined that the deep cut required for the garden would endanger the monument, and it was never realized. Beyond the obelisk is the greensward flanked by parallel carriage paths, rows of elms, and classical buildings. These features, which appeared here for the first time, would become reality in the decades to follow.

recommendation, and the base was installed in 1908 in what was then the Botanic Garden. This action drew vigorous protests, since it required the destruction of numerous large trees.

In 1909, shortly before his death, Charles McKim wrote to Lawrence White, the son of his late partner, Stanford White:

When you reach these shores again, you must go to Washington and see the Senate and House Office buildings—immense structures of white marble flanking the Capitol—the work of Carrère & Hastings. They are really fine, and worthy to stand where they are. Burnham's immense rail-

way station, the new Museum, the Department of Agriculture and the Grant Monument—all of marble and built along the lines in accordance with the Park Commission plan. As Mr. Root says: "Enough pegs driven to make it impossible for anybody to pull them up."[23]

Indeed, the McMillan Plan had been set in stone. Much had been achieved within just a few years, but two of the most important steps toward the fulfillment of the plan were still to come: the creation of the Commission of Fine Arts and the construction of the Lincoln Memorial.

In 1902, Congress created a commission to plan a memorial to Abraham Lincoln, but the effort went nowhere. Although Representative Joseph Cannon of Illinois supported a memorial, he vehemently opposed the McMillan Commission's preferred site in unfinished Potomac Park (see pages 110–111) because he perceived it as a malarial wasteland unworthy of Lincoln's memory. The McMillan Plan was anathema to him, both because of his fiscal conservatism and because its creation by the Senate bypassed the House, which he took as a personal affront. As chairman of the House Appropriations Committee, he held considerable power. In 1903 he became Speaker of the House, and his near dictatorial control of that body made him a formidable opponent. Cannon consistently fought the commission's recommendations—he opposed locating the Grant Memorial in the Botanic Garden and supported the secretary of agriculture in his fight with McKim over the location of the Department of Agriculture building.

The arrival in 1909 of the centennial of Lincoln's birth motivated Congress to once again consider a memorial to the Great Emancipator. There were two other serious proposals, besides the one that appeared in the McMillan Plan. One was a ceremonial highway between Washington and Gettysburg, which was enthusiastically backed by real estate and transportation interests. The other was an expansion of the Capitol grounds with some sort of memorial located between the Capitol and Union Station. The threat that this latter scheme posed to the McMillan Plan spurred President Roosevelt to create the Council of Fine Arts. The council would advise the federal government on new buildings, and its members would be selected by Roosevelt himself.

Congress refused to fund Roosevelt's council on the grounds that it was established by executive order, an act that had no legal standing, but it was really a reflection of a broader conflict within the Republican Party, between Roosevelt and the free-spending Progressives on the one hand, and Cannon and the fiscal conservatives on the other. In March 1909, William Howard Taft succeeded Roosevelt as president. Like his predecessor, Taft was an enthusiastic supporter of the McMillan Plan. With Taft's backing, Congress passed legislation in 1910 establishing the Commission of Fine Arts (CFA), an expert panel that would give the federal government advice on the location and design of statues, fountains, and monuments in the District of Columbia.

Taft picked men who would vigorously champion the McMillan Plan. They included Daniel Burnham and Frederick Law Olmsted Jr., the surviving members of the McMillan Commission, and Charles Moore, who had been its secretary. He also appointed sculptor Daniel Chester French, who had worked on the Chicago fair; painter Francis D. Millet; and Cass Gilbert and Thomas Hastings, two of the most prominent classical architects in the country.

The authority of the Commission of Fine Arts was expanded over the years by executive order and through additional legislation. Taft soon extended the CFA's domain to include the design of federal buildings in the District, requiring federal officials to submit their plans to the CFA for *advice*. In 1930, Congress passed the Shipstead-Luce Act, which requires that any plans for semipublic or private buildings that adjoin important public buildings or parks in the capital be submitted to the CFA for its advice, as well. The 1986 Commemorative Works Act requires commission *approval* for all memorials on Park Service and General Services Administration land in the city.

Currently, the Commission of Fine Arts holds public meetings once a month and reviews proposals for new monuments, federal buildings, and other projects. The commission can suggest changes to a design, and its advice is rarely ignored. In the case of memorials covered by the Commemorative Works Act, its approval of the site and design is mandatory. Frequently, the design process becomes a collaboration between the CFA and the architect. Or, as in the case of the World War II Memorial, the commission can effectively select the site.

IN FEBRUARY 1911, Congress created the Lincoln Memorial Commission to plan and execute a memorial to the 16th president. The commissioners included Taft and six prominent members of Congress, none of whom were particularly knowledgeable in matters of art. At its first meeting, Taft became chairman, and at his initiative, the commission asked the CFA for advice on the site and a method for choosing an architect.

The CFA predictably recommended the Potomac Park site proposed by the McMillan Commission and suggested that architect Henry Bacon be commissioned to design the memorial. Bacon had been an assistant to Charles McKim at his firm McKim, Mead and White, and he could be relied upon to produce a design that would be sympathetic to the one in the McMillan Plan. Bacon was not well known to the public, but he was highly regarded within his profession.

In August 1911, the Lincoln Memorial Commission asked Bacon to prepare some designs for the Potomac Park site. Joseph Cannon, now a member of the memorial commission, was as opposed as ever to that location. At his instigation, the commission engaged architect John Russell Pope for designs to fit two alternative sites, one at Meridian Hill and the other at the Soldier's Home. Both sites were on hilltops on the outskirts of Washington that offered broad views of the city.

The memorial commission considered the designs in December 1911. In general, the press and the country's artistic elite supported Bacon's scheme, which was very similar to the memorial as it was eventually built, while Pope's proposals enjoyed some popular support. The one for the Soldier's Home was particularly dramatic, with an immense circular colonnade surrounding a seated figure of Lincoln under an open sky. Glenn Brown, who had lobbied for the creation of the CFA and the Lincoln Memorial Commission, became a strong proponent of Bacon's plan.

Early in 1912, the memorial commission settled on Potomac Park. Pope was asked to adapt his scheme for the Soldier's Home to that site, while Bacon was allowed to revise his design. Bacon's scheme was ultimately approved, and construction began in 1913. He also designed the landscape setting of the memorial, while the CFA determined the dimensions of the reflecting pool and the details of the landscaping on each side. The memorial was dedicated in 1922, marking the fulfillment of the most important component of the McMillan Plan.

Congress undertook the construction of the Memorial Bridge that same year. Together with an adjacent set of steps leading to the Potomac (known as the Water Gate) and the entrance to Rock Creek Parkway, the bridge formed an ensemble that closely followed the recommendations of the McMillan Plan. In 1923, the Freer Gallery of Art opened on the Mall, and many other important public buildings were constructed in the city's central area, all of them in conformity with the McMillan Plan.

Architect John Russell Pope suggested this pyramid as one of several alternative schemes for the Lincoln Memorial.

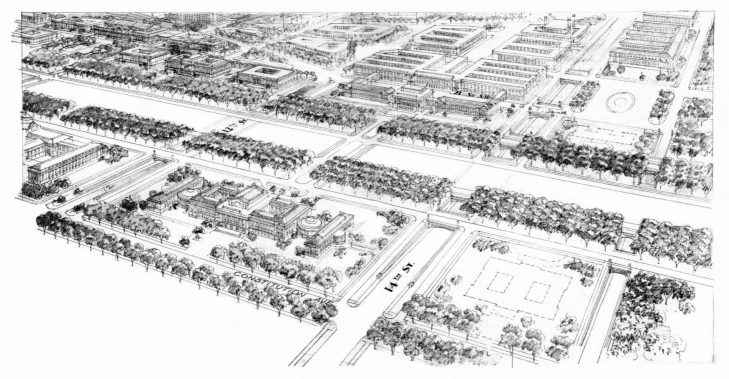

This rendering, published in the 1931 annual report of the National Capital Park and Planning Commission, depicts the Mall of the future. Twelfth, Fourteenth, and Fifteenth streets run through tunnels under the greensward, but the plans for the Fifteenth Street tunnel were soon abandoned because it would have destabilized the Washington Monument. The building in the left foreground with twin rotundas is a hypothetical art gallery for the Smithsonian Institution, occupying the present-day site of the National Museum of American History. The Smithsonian Castle has been removed in this vision of the future, but the greensward and rows of elms were soon realized.

THE NEXT IMPORTANT STEP in the fulfillment of the McMillan Plan was the completion of the Mall between First and Fourteenth streets. As late as 1930, the picturesque nineteenth-century landscaping was largely intact, even as Beaux-Arts buildings sprang up incongruously among the Victorian plantings. Before the end of the decade, the Mall would be transformed into a far more open space. The old Victorian Mall was plowed under and replaced with classically inspired landscaping that was thought to be in keeping with the intentions of Peter L'Enfant.

In its 1902 plan, the McMillan Commission proposed planting a carpet of grass 300 feet wide along the main axis of the Mall, flanked by four rows of elms. Four parallel drives would be laid under the trees from Third Street to Fifteenth Street. In the 1910s and '20s, the Army Corps of Engineers began to carry out the work

in a limited and piecemeal fashion. The plans were drawn up by the engineers and reviewed by the landscape architect member of the CFA, first Frederick Law Olmsted Jr., until 1918, and then James Greenleaf.[24] The inner drives between Third and Seventh streets were partially completed, some trees were planted, and the temporary government office buildings constructed in 1918 were sited to be as unobstructive as possible.

In 1924, Congress created the National Capital Park Commission, largely at the instigation of civic groups who believed that a more beautiful city would promote business and protect property values. Initially, its role was to acquire parklands as recommended by the McMillan Commission. However, two years later, Congress expanded the commission's duties to include planning for the Washington metropolitan area. With "Planning" added to its name

Top. The Mall was regraded in the 1930s, requiring an enormous amount of fill.

Bottom. In this 1937 view of the Mall from the Washington Monument, the newly planted elms and the four new parallel drives are clearly visible.

to reflect its new role, the National Capital Park and Planning Commission (NCPPC) was charged with developing a comprehensive plan encompassing public buildings, transportation, zoning, and other aspects of the capital's development. Since that time, the planning commission has met monthly to review and approve any plans for federal land in the city, among its many other duties. Where its jurisdiction overlaps with the CFA, the two agencies try to coordinate their actions.

The NCPPC began work on detailed landscaping plans for the Mall in 1926. The commission's firm support of the McMillan Plan was assured, since there was a great deal of continuity between the commission and those who had protected the 1902 plan during the previous decades. Landscape architect Frederick Law Olmsted Jr., the only surviving member of the McMillan Commission and a former member of the Commission of Fine Arts, was now an NCPPC commissioner. Milton Medary Jr., another member of the NCPPC, had served on the Fine Arts Commission as well.

Olmsted and Thomas C. Jeffers, a landscape architect on the staff of the NCPPC, were the principal authors of the commission's plans for the Mall, basing their work on the earlier plans by the McMillan Commission and the Army Corps of Engineers. Through the early 1930s, they devoted considerable attention to the important question of how the Mall should be regraded. In 1901, McMillan Commission members Olmsted and Charles McKim concluded that it would be impractical to create a geometrically perfect surface on the Mall and instead chose to use the natural contours to create an undulating effect. They believed that the natural differences in grade were too large to correct without leaving some distracting imperfections, and the wholesale destruction of mature trees might create enough opposition to doom the plan. Besides, during their visit to Europe, they had seen park avenues where an undulating surface had produced a pleasing effect.

By the time that the NCPPC revisited the question of grading, conditions had changed considerably. Traffic congestion was a growing problem, and it was sure to be exacerbated by the Federal Triangle, to the north of the Mall, which was begun in 1928. To reduce traffic across the Mall, the NCPPC decided to run Twelfth and Fourteenth streets below grade, with the four parallel drives passing overhead on bridges. Depressing the two streets could wait until some future date when funds were available, but for the grading to be consistent with that goal, it would need to slope gradually upward from Third Street to Fourteenth Street. Considerable fill would be required west of Twelfth Street.[25]

In March 1929, Congress passed legislation authorizing work on the "Mall parkway," as well as Union Square (now the site of the Capitol Reflecting Pool) and new parkland between the Capitol and Union Station. Congress specified that work should follow the L'Enfant and McMillan plans, with any modifications recommended by the NCPPC.[26] This legislation marked the first time that Congress had formally acknowledged its acceptance of the McMillan Plan.

The NCPPC hoped that the project would be completed in 1932, for the celebration of the bicentennial of George Washington's birth, but the appropriations were small and progress was slow. Work began at the west end of the Mall, and by early 1931, the drive in front of the new Agriculture Department headquarters was finished. The work was supervised by the Office of Public Buildings and Public Parks of the National Capital (see page 49), an independent agency headed by Ulysses S. Grant III, a military officer and a grandson of the Civil War general. Grant was an *ex officio* member of the NCPPC as well and played an important role in city planning at that time, especially through his connections with the White House.

The temporary buildings constructed during World War I were a persistent impediment to the completion of the Mall. These could not be demolished until permanent quarters could be found for the departments they housed. The tempos, as they were called, were concentrated on the Mall between Fourth and Ninth streets, and most were gone by the end of 1935. Another obstacle was the old Botanic Garden, which straddled the Mall between First and Third streets. When Congress passed legislation in 1926 to move the garden, the Commission of Fine Arts considered it the most important step toward the completion of the Mall since the railroad tracks had

Top. When the weather was cold enough, Washingtonians enjoyed ice skating on the 2,027-foot-long reflecting pool, seen here in 1932. Skating was allowed until the early 1980s.

Bottom. Cycling in West Potomac Park, near the site of the present-day Roosevelt Bridge, 1942. In the background is a statue of William Jennings Bryan, which was later moved to Salem, Illinois, Bryan's birthplace.

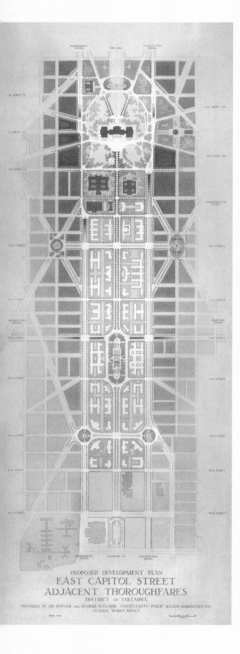

PROPOSED DEVELOPMENT PLAN
EAST CAPITOL STREET
ADJACENT THOROUGHFARES
DISTRICT OF COLUMBIA
PREPARED BY JAY DOWNER AND GILMORE D. CLARKE CONSULTANTS PUBLIC ROADS ADMINISTRATION
FEDERAL WORKS AGENCY

been removed.[27] The old conservatory, by that time dangerously deteriorated, was razed in 1934.

Work continued on the outer drives in 1932. At the same time, the Mall was filled and graded to produce a flat surface. The fill dirt was hauled from the nearby Federal Triangle, where excavations for new government buildings were underway.

In 1933, the National Park Service assumed responsibility for the Mall. As secretary of the Interior Department, Harold Ickes oversaw the Park Service. He was also administrator of the Public Works Administration (PWA), a New Deal agency established by Franklin Roosevelt to fight unemployment by sponsoring public works projects. In September 1933, Ickes approved an allocation of $600,000 by the PWA for completion of the Mall work, far more than had been spent previously. The amount would grow to more than $1 million.

With the additional funds, work proceeded rapidly. The grading continued, and rows of elms were planted. Most of the land on the Mall that was controlled by other agencies was transferred to the Park Service. Four blocks of privately owned buildings along Missouri and Maine avenues (see page 62), carved out of the public grounds in 1822, were repurchased by the federal government and cleared. At Union Square, the site of the old Botanic Garden, some of the historic trees were transplanted, and dozens of old English boxwoods were installed around a broad plaza.

All of this activity required the removal of many old trees, much to the consternation of tree-loving Washingtonians. In May 1935, Representative Daniel Reed of New York complained that a beautiful park was being transformed into a wasteland, but most of the damage was already done.[28] Progress on the Mall also eliminated numerous baseball fields, football gridirons, tennis courts, and volleyball courts.

By October 1935, the four drives along the greensward were essentially finished. A year later, Park Service Director Arno Cammerer reported that the project was 90 percent complete and that only some miscellaneous work remained.[29]

In 1937, the NCPPC named the four drives after the first four presidents: Washington, Adams, Jefferson, and Madison. The commission named the drive closest to Constitution Avenue for Madison because he was the father of the Constitution, while the one nearest Independence Avenue became Jefferson Drive because Jefferson was the author of the Declaration of Independence. The two inner drives became Washington Drive (on the north) and Adams Drive.[30]

Now one of the most important components of the McMillan Plan was in place. The picturesque Victorian landscaping was gone, and the vista between the Capitol and the Washington Monument, planned by L'Enfant but obscured for many years, was restored. The four drives, the eight rows of elm trees, and the greensward—almost a mile long and 300 feet wide—emphasized the importance of the Capitol and the Washington Monument and the axial relationship between them. All that remained was to tear down the last few Victorian buildings. The prevailing view held that the Castle should be saved, if possible, by moving it off the Mall. The Arts and Industries building and the Army Medical Museum were thought to be eyesores that should be razed as soon as practicable.

Another important plan developed by the NCPPC would have extended the Mall from the Capitol east to the Anacostia River. This project had its genesis in a memorial to Theodore Roosevelt that was proposed for the Tidal Basin. When it became apparent that it would not be built, a group of Washington businessmen went to Ulysses S. Grant III, hoping to save the memorial for the city. Grant proposed a giant coliseum as an appropriate memorial to Roosevelt, an avid sportsman. The stadium, which could be used for football games, Olympic events, and other purposes, would stand at the foot of East Capitol Street on the west bank of the Anacostia. It would be two miles east of the Capitol, balancing the Lincoln Memorial, which is two miles west of the Capitol.

The plans, which were published in 1929, were drawn up by Charles W. Eliot II, the NCPPC's director of planning. To form an appropriate connection between the stadium and the Capitol, East Capitol Street was to be transformed into the Avenue of the States. This would be realized by clearing the blocks facing East Capitol Street for its entire 24-block length, 48 blocks in all. Each block would have a building built by one of the states, which would house exhibits on its history and showcase the accomplishments of its citizens, its agricultural and manufactured products, and so on. The buildings could feature indigenous materials, such as Indiana limestone for the Indiana building or redwood paneling for the California building. Midway along the Avenue of the States would be Colonial Square, surrounded by the buildings of the 13 original states. It was an idea that had originated with Peter L'Enfant, who had suggested that 15 squares around the city be dedicated to the individual states, which could use them as sites for monuments to their most illustrious citizens.[31]

In 1941, the NCPPC considered an even more ambitious plan for East Capitol Street. A scheme by Jay Downer and Gilmore Clarke (see the rendering on the opposite page), consultants to the NCPPC, was enthusiastically received by the commission in April of that year. An immense area between what is now Constitution and Independence avenues, from the Capitol to the Anacostia, would be cleared and filled with federal office buildings. The "Eastern Rectangle," as it was called, was clearly inspired by the success of the recently completed Federal Triangle. The proposed buildings would have provided office space for tens of thousands of federal workers, saving the government millions of dollars a year paid for rented space.[32]

NCPPC architect William Partridge devised a similar scheme for the Eastern Rectangle as part of his plan for Washington's central area that was published in September 1941. Partridge proposed putting large office buildings along Independence and Constitution avenues and smaller structures, such as private museums or state buildings, on East Capitol Street. Nothing ever came of the scheme, although the D.C. Stadium (now RFK Stadium) opened in 1961 on the site

intended for the Roosevelt coliseum. East Capitol Street, which was considered a blighted area in the 1930s, would be rehabilitated, making it a less attractive site for wholesale redevelopment.[33]

Work began on the National Gallery of Art in 1937, on the site of the old Baltimore and Potomac Railroad Station. The building is 782 feet long, longer than the U.S. Capitol, and it required closing Sixth Street where it crossed the Mall. The gallery and the core of its collection were the gift of banker and financier Andrew Mellon, who had served as secretary of the treasury during the 1920s. John Russell Pope, the building's architect, designed the Jefferson Memorial as well, which was constructed beside the Tidal Basin between 1938 and 1943 (see pages 118–119).

During World War II, the federal government filled the Mall and West Potomac Park with temporary office buildings for government war workers. Unlike the temporary buildings of World War I, which were concrete, the World War II tempos were built of wood. They were meant to be demolished immediately after the war, but the Cold War intervened, and demand for office space remained high. The tempos became a persistent eyesore, enduring into the 1960s in defiance of all efforts to remove them. The last were razed in 1970.

The 1930s and '40s were a time of stagnation for the Smithsonian, and it struggled along, poorly funded. The appointment of Leonard Carmichael as secretary in 1953 ushered in a new era, as Carmichael was able to increase the Smithsonian's appropriations from Congress dramatically. Work began in 1958 on the Museum of History and Technology, now the National Museum of American History. It opened in 1964, a showcase for American accomplishments during some of the darkest days of the Cold War.

The American History Museum was just the first of a number of museums to be built on the Mall in a period of vast expansion for the Smithsonian that continues to the present day. The Hirshhorn Museum and Sculpture Garden opened in 1974; the National Air and Space Museum, in 1976; the Sackler Gallery and the National Museum of African Art, in 1987; and the National Museum of the American Indian, in 2004.

OPPOSITE. Before World War II, planning agencies considered several proposals for extending the Mall to the east, from the Capitol to the Anacostia River. This 1941 scheme, oriented here with north to the right, would have filled the area between Constitution and Independence avenues with federal office buildings.

The public swimming pools on the Mall were open during the summer, between 1910 and 1935. They were located just to the northwest of the Washington Monument.

AFTER THE NATIONAL Park Service completed the landscaping of the Mall in the 1930s, there were no major initiatives to improve the Mall for almost three decades. During World War II, the nation focused on the war effort. After the war, planners became occupied with broader regional issues, as suburban growth accelerated and the city's monumental core became only a small part of the overall picture. In 1952, an act of Congress reorganized the National Capital Park and Planning Commission. The word "Park" was dropped from its name, reflecting a decreased emphasis on developing the city's park system. In its *Year 2000 Policies Plan* for the city, published in 1961, the National Capital Planning Commission (NCPC) dealt with the Mall in only a few sentences, describing it as a completed composition.

The Washington Mall Master Plan of 1966 was the first major plan for the improvement of the Mall since the McMillan Plan and the last to propose significant changes to the park. It was also known as the SOM Plan, after its principal author, the architectural firm of Skidmore, Owings and Merrill, or the Owings plan, after Nathaniel Owings, a partner in the firm and the plan's most enthusiastic spokesman. Unlike the McMillan Plan, perhaps half of whose proposals for the monumental core were completed, little of the SOM Plan was ever implemented.

The SOM Plan had its origins in the dismal condition of Pennsylvania Avenue, the city's principal boulevard and the site of inaugural parades. The south side of the avenue between the White House and the Capitol had been redeveloped in the 1930s as part of the Federal Triangle project, but the north side was lined with nineteenth-century commercial buildings, many of them in poor condition. At the impetus of Presidents Kennedy and Johnson, a presidential commission, chaired by Owings, created a plan for the improvement of the avenue. The recommendations, made public in 1964, included a huge National Square at Fifteenth Street, which would have required razing the Willard Hotel; a stronger Eighth Street axis, from the old Patent Office through the Mall; and a reflecting pool on the Mall where Pennsylvania Avenue joined the grounds of the Capitol.

Secretary of the Interior Stuart L. Udall became convinced that a complementary set of plans for the Mall was needed, and the National Park Service contracted with SOM in March 1965. The work was done in SOM's San Francisco office, principally by architects Charles Bassett, Dan Kiley, and John Woodbridge, although Owings and many other staff members were involved. Kiley worked as a consultant to SOM; although his name is not widely known to the public, he is considered by many to be the most important American landscape architect of the twentieth century. The SOM Plan was first shown to the public in December, then formally presented to the Park Service in 1966.

The most striking aspect of the new plan was the complete banishment of automobiles from the Mall. All of the cross streets would be carried through tunnels, except for Third Street, which would become a curved Ceremonial Drive. Tourists would park at remote locations or in several new underground garages. The only way to see the Mall would be on foot or from tour buses that would circulate through the park. SOM also proposed tripling the number of trees on the Mall. The four rows of elms on each side of the central greensward would be interplanted with new trees to deepen the shade. Magnolias would be added outside the rows of elms; on the inside, flanking the greensward, one row of flowering chestnuts would be added to each side. The greensward would thus be narrowed—a surprising choice, given that this was one of the most sacred aspects of the McMillan Plan, and one that its proponents vigorously defended. There was a perception that the Mall was a dull and lifeless place, and a key goal of the SOM Plan was to humanize it. Under the shade of the trees would be a wide variety of new attractions, including cafés, kiosks, bandstands, carousels, and playgrounds that would draw people to the Mall, enhancing its vitality.

The plan catered to tourists, whose numbers were expected to grow radically in the coming years, and shunted local commuters into tunnels that passed under the Mall. The plan accommodated the Inner Loop, or Interstate 695 as it was sometimes known, an inner beltway that would have devastated the city had it been completed.

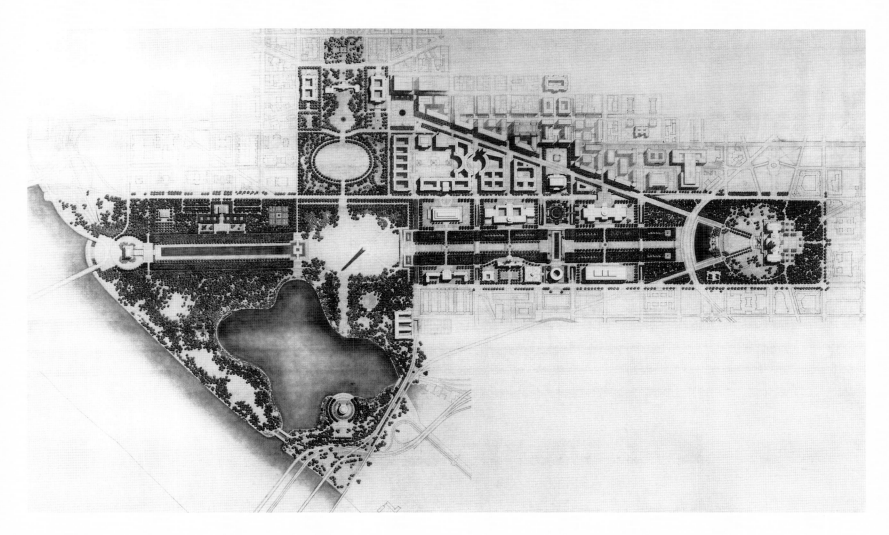

The only parts that were actually built were the Southeast and Southwest freeways and a short stretch (now Interstate 66) near the Kennedy Center. The remainder, which would have cut through Dupont Circle and many other city neighborhoods following Florida Avenue, was stopped by community opposition. The Inner Loop would have cut through West Potomac Park, passing under the Lincoln Memorial and connecting with the Southwest Freeway and the Fourteenth Street Bridge. One variant of the plan ran the highway through a tunnel under the Tidal Basin, while another would have built a depressed roadway through the park. Owings urged the completion of the tunnel because it furthered his goal of removing cars from the surface of the Mall.

Architect Nathaniel Owings (right) shows his 1966 plan for the Mall to Lady Bird Johnson and her First Lady's Committee for a More Beautiful Capital. Between them stands Secretary of the Interior Stewart L. Udall. The others are, from the left, Elizabeth Rowe, chairman of the National Capital Planning Commission; Margaret McNamara, wife of the secretary of defense; State Department official Katie Louchheim; businessman C. William Martin Jr.; philanthropist Laurance S. Rockefeller; and architect John M. Woodbridge.

In 1966, the Commission of Fine Arts rejected some of the key aspects of the SOM Plan, effectively dooming it. Chief among these was the concept of the Mall as a carless preserve, the centerpiece of the plan. The commission also disliked the narrowed greensward and suggested that the proposed plantings were too dense overall. Finally, it rejected a visitor center and overlook that was planned for the Washington Monument grounds near Fourteenth Street. The commission felt that its location on the main axis would interrupt the long green panel that was such an important part of the Mall.

The most direct result of the SOM Plan was the Capitol Reflecting Pool, and Owings facilitated its construction. A new interstate highway known as the Center Leg of the Inner Loop Freeway (now Interstate 395) was supposed to pass through a tunnel underneath the Mall near Third Street. The tunnel required a broad curve to the west to avoid some venerable trees, which couldn't survive in the thin soil above it. Owings successfully convinced the myriad government agencies involved that developing the pool would negate the need to preserve the trees, and the tunnel could be straightened. That would

save $2 million, enough to pay for the pool. Work on the project, which included the tunnel and a new building for the Department of Labor north of the Mall, began in 1968.[34]

In 1973, Skidmore, Owings and Merrill took another look at the Mall for the National Park Service. The resulting 1976 Development Plan was much more modest in scope than the 1966 plan. It sought to beautify the parks in the city's core in time for the bicentennial and make the area more comfortable and convenient for the many anticipated visitors. It only included elements of the 1966 plan that could be completed for the bicentennial, but it suggested that other parts of that plan, such as tunneling the cross streets under the Mall, could be finished later. The 1976 plan retained the Ceremonial Drive at Third Street (which was never built) and the narrowed greensward. It also reflected new plans for Constitution Gardens, the National Gallery of Art Sculpture Garden, and the Hirshhorn Museum and Sculpture Garden, which was then under construction.[35]

A separate, more detailed, rehabilitation plan focused on the Mall between Third and Fourteenth streets. Congress provided funds, and work began in late 1975. Washington and Adams drives, which bordered the inside of the greensward, were closed to traffic and replaced with gravel paths (a photograph of Adams Drive appears on page 101). Fragments of Sixth and Thirteenth streets were removed as well. The Park Service added lamps, benches, kiosks, and trash cans. The rehabilitation plan originally included the two rows of trees that would have narrowed the greensward. Owings was passionate about the trees and had persuaded the CFA to accept them. However, the NCPC rejected the trees, and the Commission of Fine Arts followed suit and reversed its decision.

Although plans to run the cross streets through tunnels dated back to the 1920s, tunnels under Ninth and Twelfth streets were the only ones to be completed. Besides helping to beautify the Mall (the Park Service contributed funds toward this purpose), they were intended to relieve traffic congestion by connecting downtown with the new Southwest Freeway and the Fourteenth Street Bridge. The Twelfth Street tunnel was completed in 1962, and the Ninth Street tunnel, in 1971.

COUNTLESS DEMONSTRATIONS and gatherings have been held on the Mall in recent years, but it was the March on Washington for Jobs and Freedom that set the standard. Held on August 28, 1963, it has became the best-known demonstration in American history, and most every mass event on the Mall since that time has been inspired by it or measured against it. Martin Luther King Jr.'s "I Have a Dream" speech, the climactic event of the march, is a defining moment of the Civil Rights movement.

The March on Washington was organized by a coalition of Civil Rights groups and labor unions. Its purpose was to add momentum to the national push for Civil Rights legislation and to encourage the creation of a large-scale jobs program. Working in close cooperation with the Kennedy administration, the march's organizers decided to confine the event to the Mall. Participants would assemble at the Washington Monument and march in two groups down Constitution and Independence avenues to the Lincoln Memorial. Besides the practical considerations of managing such a large crowd, marching past the White House or the Capitol was perceived as being too confrontational. To have the desired impact, the organizers hoped to have at least 100,000 participants, and toward that goal, they staged a national advertising campaign.

On the day of the march, the participants numbered more than 200,000. The *Washington Post* estimated that the crowd was 70 percent black and commended the order and dignity of the marchers. At the Washington Monument, participants picked up preprinted signs as entertainers performed on a stage; Joan Baez sang "We Shall Overcome." After the crowd had moved to the Lincoln Memorial, Marian Anderson began the program by singing the national anthem. The organizers of the march addressed the demonstrators in turn. Other speakers included Rosa Parks and Myrlie Evers, the widow of Medgar Evers. The climax came at the end when King gave his now-immortal speech. He was supposed to talk for only four minutes, but he abandoned his prepared text and spoke for 16 minutes. With his powerful oratory, the 34-year-old Baptist minister articulated his dream to the huge crowd: "I still have a dream. It is a dream deeply rooted in the American dream.

I have a dream that one day this nation will rise up and live out the true meaning of its creed: 'We hold these truths to be self-evident, that all men are created equal.'"

Afterward, King and the other organizers met with President John F. Kennedy in the White House. The attention that this demonstration received from the president and the media is almost inconceivable today. It was broadcast live in the United States and around the world on television, and the president himself watched it in the White House. The march was even scheduled to be shown in the Soviet Union, but the broadcast was canceled at the last moment. The effectiveness of the march is still debated, but it is widely credited with contributing to the passage of landmark Civil Rights legislation during the Johnson administration.

The 1963 March on Washington brought a crowd estimated at 200,000 to the Mall. Martin Luther King Jr.'s "I Have a Dream" speech, delivered from the steps of the Lincoln Memorial, became a defining event of the Civil Rights era.

The entire AIDS Memorial Quilt was on display on the Washington Monument grounds over an October weekend in 1992. The quilt comprises sewn three- by six-foot panels, each of which honors a person who died of AIDS. There were more than 20,000 panels, covering 15 acres. The entire quilt has been displayed five times, and each took place in Washington. The last was in 1996.

Perhaps the most memorable mass demonstration on the Mall since that time was the farmers' protest in 1979. On February 5, thousands of supporters of the American Agricultural Movement converged on the Mall from staging areas outside the city. The farmers drove hundreds of slow-moving tractors down many of the city's most important arteries during the morning rush hour, causing what was described as the worst traffic jam in the city's history. The protesters met with members of Congress and the administration, seeking increased price supports for farm products, but they received few, if any, concessions.

Fearing a repeat of the chaotic scene during the evening rush hour, District police surrounded about 625 tractors on the Mall with trucks and buses. The protesting farmers remained boxed in on the Mall for a month, causing severe damage as they rode about on their tractors. Much of the sod was destroyed, as were numerous trees, kiosks, and benches. The protesters made occasional forays into the city, causing traffic snarls and raising the ire of District residents. After negotiations with city officials, most of the protesters were gone by the second week of March 1979.

In the decades since the March on Washington, the Mall has become the preferred stage for national rallies and demonstrations. As these events have become routine, they have attracted less and less attention from the public and the media. Their organizers work closely with the National Park Service, and they are orderly affairs. Sometimes the rallies do not have a specific goal such as influencing legislation, but the demonstrators do hope to energize a movement and build solidarity among its members, much as the March on Washington did.

The Million Man March, held on October 16, 1995, is one of the most important demonstrations of recent decades. It was organized by Louis Farrakhan, leader of the Nation of Islam, a black separatist movement. Farrakhan brought a vast throng of black men to the Mall for a day of personal atonement and reaffirmation. The marchers were encouraged to take charge of their lives and communities, to become politically active, and to fight violence and drugs. Many were ambivalent about Farrakhan himself, praising the march while distancing themselves from his sometimes extreme ideology. As the marchers listened to a day of speeches, many said that the feeling of camaraderie and solidarity was intense, and some noted that the crowd seemed as much focused on itself as it was on the speakers. The culmination of the event was a speech by Farrakhan, but many of the participants left as he rambled on for more than two hours.

Afterward, the National Park Service estimated the attendance at 400,000, while the march's organizers said the true figure was well over a million. The size of the turnout became the measure of the march's success, and Farrakhan threatened to sue the Park Service over its estimate. Since then, the Park Service has declined to make public estimates of crowd sizes. The Million Man March spawned such imitators as the Million Mom March and started a debate on the impact of similar mass events on the Mall, especially on the health of the grass and trees.

THE CROWDS at the 1963 March on Washington stretched from the Lincoln Memorial to the Washington Monument along both sides of the reflecting pool. Close inspection of photographs of the event shows that many of the temporary office buildings from World War I and World War II were still standing. By the end of 1970, the last of these had been razed, many of them for new Smithsonian museums. Smithsonian Secretary Leonard Carmichael began expanding the institution in the late 1950s with the Museum of History and Technology (now the National Museum of American History). It was only the first of more than a half dozen new museums that would transform the National Mall into the home of the largest museum complex in the world.

The National Museum of the American Indian, which opened in 2004, took what was widely considered to be the last available vacant site for a museum on the Mall. A century earlier, the McMillan Commission had recommended flanking the greensward with two rows of museums and buildings dedicated to science. Over the decades, the CFA and the NCPC guarded the Mall against encroachment by other government buildings, successfully fending off several attempts to construct departmental office buildings there before World War II. With the completion of the Indian Museum, an important part of the McMillan Plan had been fulfilled.

Another important change in recent decades was the establishment of four major memorials on prominent sites in West Potomac Park. The turning point was the construction of the Vietnam Veterans Memorial in 1982. It was the first new memorial on the Mall in nearly 40 years—the last had been the Jefferson Memorial in 1943—and its distinctive design was tremendously influential. Its broad success inspired other groups to establish their own monuments, notably the Korean War Veterans Memorial (1995) and the World War II Memorial (2004).

Maya Lin's design, spare and abstract, most likely would have been passed up in favor of a more conventional design if the competition jury had not included numerous architectural professionals. While most of the other entries recycled classical motifs, Lin's design offered something new and different. It was the first suc-

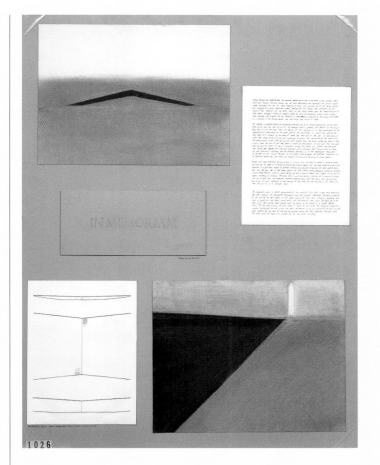

Maya Lin's winning entry in the 1981 competition for the Vietnam Veterans Memorial included two pastel sketches and a handwritten description of her proposal. Lin's modernist design, very different from any of the other entries, immediately seized the imagination of the judges.

cessful modern design for a memorial in Washington. (Two modern designs for the FDR Memorial had been rejected in the 1960s as too massive and unsympathetic to their site in West Potomac Park.) The granite wall, so affecting in the Vietnam memorial, has reappeared in various forms in most subsequent memorials on the Mall. And, while some earlier memorials had a large landscaping component—most notably the Lincoln Memorial—recent designs have relied on it much more than past schemes. Landscaping solutions tend to use considerably more land, as well.

In 1986, Congress passed the Commemorative Works Act,[36] which codified a procedure for adding memorials in Washington. The legislation was a response to a dramatic increase in proposals for new commemorative works in the wake of the popular success of the Vietnam Veterans Memorial. As a practical matter, it had little effect on the steps that one needed to follow to place a memorial on the Mall, since the procedure was already well established. Rather, the act prescribed what could be memorialized and where: Area I, which included the Mall, West Potomac Park, and the immediate area, would be reserved for commemorative works whose subject is "of preeminent historical and lasting significance to the Nation." Area II, which included the District of Columbia and its environs outside Area I, would be for memorials whose subject had "lasting historical significance to the American people."

Any group that hopes to build a memorial on Park Service or General Services Administration land in Washington first needs to obtain authorization from Congress through legislation, and it is up to Congress to determine whether the subject is "of preeminent historical and lasting significance to the Nation." Congress can authorize construction in Area I, but the sponsoring group chooses the site in consultation with the National Park Service if it plans to build on Park Service land. The site and design must be approved by the Commission of Fine Arts, the National Capital Planning Commission, and the secretary of the Interior (who oversees the Park Service). Finally, the secretary of the Interior must approve detailed plans before construction can begin.

Previously, the CFA had the right to *advise* on new memorials, although its advice was rarely ignored; the new legislation gave it the authority to *approve* all commemorative works. The NCPC already had approval authority over all construction on federal land in Washington, so its role was essentially unchanged by the new law. The two commissions have separate monthly meetings, and typically, a memorial proposal will appear before the commissions repeatedly as a site is chosen and the design is refined.

Although the Commemorative Works Act provided some structure to the process of adding to the Mall, it did little to stem the tide of proposals for new memorials. The proposed subjects included Martin Luther King Jr., the U.S. Air Force, disabled American war veterans, Dwight Eisenhower, Ronald Reagan, and even dogs who assisted the armed forces. Everyone seemed to want a prominent site on the Mall, and while the causes were worthy, many feared that Potomac Park was rapidly filling to capacity. The open spaces that provided room for recreation and an appropriate setting for memorials, such as the one to Lincoln, seemed to be on the verge of resembling a memorial theme park, as dense as an overcrowded knickknack shelf.

In 1997, the NCPC published its Extending the Legacy Plan, a roadmap for the development of the city's central area for the next century. Planners believed that the Mall was running out of available space for museums and memorials and that the best way to protect it from overbuilding was to provide attractive sites elsewhere in the city. Offered as a successor to the L'Enfant and McMillan plans, the Legacy Plan recommended recentering the city's monumental core on the Capitol by redeveloping blighted North and South Capitol streets. The removal of the Southeast–Southwest Freeway and obsolete railroad tracks south of the Mall would allow South Capitol Street to be transformed into a monumental boulevard on the scale of Pennsylvania Avenue. The terminus of South Capitol Street on the Potomac would be an ideal location for the Supreme Court, while the avenue itself would provide sites for museums and memorials. The city's underutilized waterfront, particularly the west bank of the Anacostia, would be revitalized and made accessible to the public.

In 2001, the NCPC followed up on the Legacy Plan with the Memorials and Museums Master Plan, which identified 100 sites around the city that would be appropriate for new memorials. Only 18 of the sites lay within Area I, and no others would be permitted there. Directing new memorials to sites outside the monumental core would preserve open space on the Mall and encourage the economic development of local neighborhoods.

The Memorials and Museums Master Plan introduced the Reserve, an area inside Area I where new memorial sites would be banned. The Reserve included the greensward from the Capitol Reflecting Pool to the Lincoln Memorial, and the cross axis from

Lafayette Park to the Tidal Basin. Although the plan did not carry the force of law when it was first introduced, it was the official policy of the CFA and the NCPC.

The Reserve did become law in November 2003, when Congress passed legislation amending the Commemorative Works Act.[37] New commemorative works and visitor centers would be prohibited there, except those already approved by Congress. At the same time, the Reserve was expanded to include virtually all of West Potomac Park. Congress could overrule the Commemorative Works Act simply by passing another law, as it had with the World War II Memorial, but the amended act would discourage that.

The location of the World War II Memorial was very controversial. The CFA chose the site in 1995 (see pages 96–97), but the public largely ignored the proposed memorial until the unveiling of Friedrich St. Florian's competition-winning design in 1997. Critics believed that it was too large and in the wrong place: It would block the vista between the Lincoln Memorial and the Washington Monument and act as a barrier for visitors walking between them. They argued that L'Enfant and his successors had intended the Mall to be a broad greensward clear of obstructions and called the proposed memorial an intrusion in a completed composition. Proponents of the memorial asserted that the Mall was not a historical artifact and pointed out that St. Florian had configured his design to preserve the important vista along the Mall's main axis.

In 1998, St. Florian revised his design; overall, the memorial was lower in profile and more sympathetic to the site. His new scheme

The Reserve was proposed in 2001 as a no-build zone by the National Capital Planning Commission as part of its Memorials and Museums Master Plan. In 2003, Congress gave the Reserve the force of law and expanded it to include the area indicated in red. Only a limited number of new memorials will be allowed in Area I, marked in yellow. The hatched area is the domain of the Architect of the Capitol.

The NFL Kickoff Football Festival Presented by Pepsi Vanilla, held in September 2003, was widely criticized for its commercialism. The spectacle filled the entire greensward from Third to Fourteenth streets.

retained the majestic elms flanking the Rainbow Pool; they would have been destroyed under the original proposal. In October 2000, a coalition of opposition groups filed a lawsuit against the federal officials responsible for approving the memorial, effectively blocking construction. The grounds for the suit were irregularities in the approval process, but the purpose was to delay construction while a national consensus could build against the location.

In May 2001, Congress passed legislation directing that work on the memorial begin immediately, immune to legal challenges. Critics pointed out that Congress had short-circuited the 1986 Commemorative Works Act, which it had passed to give order to the memorial-building process. Furthermore, they worried that Congress had set a terrible precedent and would routinely bypass the rigorous approval process for new additions to the Mall. Construction began that August, and the memorial was dedicated on Memorial Day 2004.

Another phenomenon that has affected the appearance of the Mall is the threat of terrorism. In 1998, after truck bomb attacks on two American embassies in Africa, the National Park Service installed a ring of concrete Jersey barriers around the base of the Washington Monument. Barriers soon appeared around the Lincoln Memorial, as well as two chain-link fences that flank the steps, preventing visitors from walking under the colonnade. The west terrace of the Capitol, which once offered one of the best views of the Mall, has been blocked off as well. Most of the other buildings on the Mall are protected by large planters and other obstacles, and a "temporary" shed was attached to the Washington Monument for screening tourists for weapons. Structures that are described as temporary do not need to be approved by the CFA or the NCPC.

Critics say that the crude security barriers and airport-style screening of visitors threaten to turn the potent symbols of freedom and democracy on the Mall into symbols of fear. They further assert that these measures portray a federal government that is obsessed with security and insensitive to architecture and history. Others respond that the threats are real. Meanwhile, efforts are underway to provide permanent security enhancements. The NCPC is promoting attractive, yet effective, vehicle barriers that use stone bollards and strengthened street furniture such as benches and lampposts. In 2005, work was completed at the Washington Monument on a vehicle barrier comprising low granite walls that form an interlocking ring about 400 feet from the base of the obelisk. The improvements also include new paths, lighting, benches, and plantings. An underground visitor center for the monument was also considered, but the National Park Service dropped the plan in 2003 after Congress denied funding for it. The visitor center, which would have been located about 400 feet to the east of the monument, would have had restrooms, educational exhibits, a bookstore, and an area for screening tourists. The proposal was widely criticized because it would have required visitors to enter the monument through a long tunnel, a potentially oppressive experience. Critics charged that the Park Service was attempting to use recent concerns over terrorism to obtain funds for a pet project that it had been promoting for decades.

ANOTHER PROBLEM facing the Mall is overuse. Every year, the National Park Service receives thousands of requests for permits to use parkland in the city for special events and demonstrations. Very few of these requests are turned down, especially for those activities protected by the First Amendment. The Mall has become the nation's center stage, a popular venue where the monuments offer a dramatic backdrop. It is the most accessible, visible park in the city, and demonstrations there promise to attract the attention of policymakers, given its proximity to Congress and the White House.

The greensward is so heavily used that the grass rarely gets a chance to recover. Many of the events require sound stages, trailers, heavy equipment, and large tents, which block the vista along the main axis of the Mall for weeks at a time, especially during the spring and summer. The federal government sponsors many events, including presidential inaugurations, the Fourth of July celebration, and the Smithsonian Folklife Festival. There are annual events, such as the Marine Corps Marathon and the Black Family Reunion, as well as demonstrations, such as the 2004 March for Women's Lives, which is said to have drawn more than 1 million people. A car repair contest sponsored by the Ford Motor Company, a French acrobatic circus, an America for Jesus Rally, and the Library of Congress's National Book Festival illustrate the diversity of activities on the Mall. In any case, Congress has not provided the National Park Service with enough funds to maintain the Mall to the highest standards, and the results are visible in the dead grass and dingy restrooms.

Perhaps the most extravagant privately sponsored event to date was the NFL Kickoff Football Festival Presented by Pepsi Vanilla, which was held on the Mall in September 2003. It was certainly the most-criticized event in recent memory, both for its commercialism and its vastness. The Park Service granted a 17-day permit for the kickoff, which filled the entire greensward from the Capitol Reflecting Pool to Fourteenth Street.

The four-day event led up to the opening game of the National Football League season on September 4. Football-related activities filled the first three days, capped by a star-studded concert on the fourth day. Afterward, fans watched the game between the Washington Redskins and the New York Jets on Jumbotron screens. Pepsi cosponsored the event with the NFL to mark the launch of Pepsi Vanilla. The size and number of the advertising signs posted on the Mall (where they would be within the sightlines of television cameras) attracted a lot of criticism. The Park Service's regulations prohibit commercial advertisements, but officials argued that the signs represented "sponsor recognition," which is permissible. In response, Senator Jeff Bingaman, from New Mexico, offered legislation that would ban advertising signs at special events on the Mall and limit the size of signs recognizing sponsors. It was signed into law in November 2003.[38]

By all accounts, the National Park Service has done an outstanding job of maintaining the elms that line the greensward—in spite of its tight budgets. There are about 600 elms on the Mall, the vast majority of which are American elms, a species chosen by the McMillan Commission for "the architectural character of its columnar trunk and delicate traceries formed by its widespreading branches" and because it is well adapted to Washington's climate.[39] Elms were first planted in large numbers along the greensward in the 1930s and since then have been replaced as necessary. Some of the original trees from that time have survived, but it is not known precisely how many.

Dutch elm disease first appeared in the United States in 1930, and in the following decades, it devastated the nation's population of elms. A fungal infection that is spread by the elm bark beetle, it was first detected on the Mall in 1950. The Park Service has been able to save the trees by regularly inspecting them and pruning or destroying those that show signs of disease. Spraying is ineffective, and finding a disease-resistant variety that looks like the American elm has been difficult. The Park Service has propagated a new disease-resistant variety, dubbed the Jefferson elm, from a single tree that was discovered on the Mall. That tree, which has survived since the 1930s, stood out from the other elms because it acquired its leaves earlier in the season and held them longer. Upon investigation, it was found to be a triploid: It has three sets of chromosomes, whereas most elms have four.

One new memorial has been approved for West Potomac Park, but has not yet been built. The Martin Luther King Jr. National Memorial, authorized by Congress in 1996, will occupy a four-acre site on the west side of the Tidal Basin. Although it is located in the Reserve, it has "grandfather" status and was allowed to go forward. In 2000, the Roma Design Group of San Francisco won a competition for the memorial's design. Their entry features a stone wall that forms an arced backdrop to the site. Between the wall and the Tidal Basin (the cherry trees will be preserved) will be a plaza, at the center of which will be a 28-foot-tall stone bearing a bas-relief sculpture of King. Sheets of water will course across the wall, which will bear quotations from King's writings and speeches. The design received preliminary approval from the CFA in 2002, and fundraising is underway. The memorial is expected to cost $100 million.

Congress authorized the Black Revolutionary War Patriots Memorial in 1986 to honor the more than 5,000 African Americans who actively supported America's bid for independence. A site in Constitution Gardens and a design were approved, but the memorial's sponsor, the Black Patriots Foundation, was unable to raise sufficient funds to begin construction. The memorial's authorization from Congress expired in 2006.

Jan Scruggs, founder and president of the Vietnam Veterans Memorial Fund, the organization that built the Vietnam Veterans Memorial, is working to establish a visitor center at the wall. Essentially a small underground museum, the center will explain the war to the public, since many visitors are now too young to remember the conflict. The project does not have the enthusiastic backing of the Park Service, but Scruggs has found support in Congress. Critics oppose adding a "mini-museum" to an already crowded Mall and fear that others will follow. Although the center will be underground, opponents believe that the necessary surface structures will mar the memorial. Proponents point out that both the Lincoln and Jefferson memorials already have exhibits concealed within their bases. Congress authorized the visitor center in 2003 as part of the legislation that barred new memorials and visitor centers from the Reserve. In September 2004, Polshek Partnership Architects was chosen as the designer.

The directors of the National Museum of African American History and Culture are planning to build on the Mall, as well. Congress established the new Smithsonian museum in 2003. The legislation allowed the Smithsonian board of regents to choose among four sites, two of which are on the Mall: the Arts and Industries building, which would have been expensive to adapt to a modern museum, and a site at the southwest corner of Constitution Avenue and Fourteenth Street. Once again, Congress had bypassed the established process for building on the Mall. Supporters of the museum ardently sought a Mall site, aware of the symbolic importance attached to anything located there. In 2006, the regents chose the Constitution Avenue site, although critics said that it was too close to the Washington Monument. Because the museum has no collection, one will have to be built over time, although objects will be available from other Smithsonian museums. Congress will fund half of the construction costs; the remainder will come from private donations.

The Vietnam Veterans Memorial was built in 1982, and its powerful design influenced many memorials that followed. The east arm of the wall points to the Washington Monument, seen here in 1999 covered in scaffolding during its restoration.

THE MALL is administered by National Mall & Memorial Parks, a division of the National Park Service whose domain comprises a number of historic sites located within L'Enfant's original city of Washington. Until it was renamed in 2005, it was known as National Capital Parks Central. As an administrative unit, the Park Service has historically defined the Mall as the rectangle bounded by Constitution and Independence avenues and First and Fourteenth streets. The popular definition includes the entire space from First Street to the Potomac River, but the term "Mall" can refer to either area.

National Mall & Memorial Parks can trace its lineage back to 1791, when George Washington appointed three commissioners to administer the new federal city. One of their responsibilities was overseeing the reservations set aside in L'Enfant's plan for the capital. These included larger parks such as the Mall, the squares scattered around the city, and the many tiny triangular parks created by Washington's oddly angled intersections.

In 1802, responsibility for the reservations went to the superintendent of the city of Washington and then, in 1816, to the commissioner of public buildings, whose wide range of responsibilities included maintaining and policing the White House, the Capitol, and other public buildings and selling lots in the city. The commissioner was directly responsible to the president until 1849, when he was placed under the newly created Department of the Interior.

In addition, the commissioner was in charge of improvements to the Mall, although progress was minimal, as the appropriations from Congress were meager. He constructed the new Botanic Garden in 1850, but various departments built the other buildings on the Mall: the Department of War, for instance, built the old Washington Armory, while a private society began work on the Washington Monument.

In 1867, the commissioner's office was abolished, and his duties were transferred to the chief of engineers of the U.S. Army, who, in turn, formed the Office of Public Buildings and Grounds to carry out the work. An engineer officer and a small staff ran the office, while most of the work was contracted out. Within the Army the post was considered a prestigious one, and the officers in charge had a wide variety of duties relating to the construction and maintenance of public buildings, parks, and monuments in the city. They frequently served on commissions created by Congress to establish memorials in the city, and in that role, they managed the architects, sculptors, and construction companies that built the memorials. They also served as military aides to the president and, consequently, had direct access to the chief executive.

The Office of Public Buildings and Grounds was itself abolished in 1925, and its duties were transferred to an independent federal agency, the Office of Public Buildings and Public Parks of the National Capital. That agency was, in turn, absorbed by the National Park Service when the latter was reorganized in 1933.

The Mall is policed by the U.S. Park Police, which began as two night watchmen hired just after the Civil War to maintain order on the grounds of the Washington Monument. Today, it serves as the urban law enforcement arm of the National Park Service. Its jurisdiction covers federal parklands in the Washington Metropolitan area, the Gateway National Recreation Area in New York City, and the Golden Gate National Recreation Area in San Francisco. The Park Police has about 720 employees, including more than 600 uniformed officers, about two-thirds of whom are in the Washington area. Its headquarters building, completed in 1963, is located in East Potomac Park. The Park Police also has a substation in East Potomac Park and horse stables on the Mall just to the south of the reflecting pool.

The greensward, looking east from Seventh Street.

OVERLEAF. Aerial view of the National Mall, 2000.

Top. William Thornton's design for the Capitol won a competition held in 1792. Thornton produced this watercolor several years later, a slightly revised version of his original design.

Bottom. The U.S. Capitol was among the buildings burned by British troops during the War of 1812.

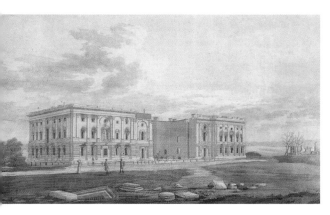

One of the most important and historic buildings in the nation, the U.S. Capitol has been the home of the legislative branch of the federal government since 1800. It visually dominates the Mall and caps one end of its main axis, the 2¼-mile line that connects the Capitol with the Lincoln Memorial. Strictly speaking though, it is not *on* the Mall. The grounds of the Capitol and the Botanic Garden are the exclusive domain of Congress and are maintained by the Architect of the Capitol, while the Mall is "owned" by the National Park Service.

The Capitol was an important part of the original plan for the city. In 1790, Congress passed the Residence Act, which established the new capital city and directed that suitable buildings be constructed by December 1800, when the federal government would move there from Philadelphia. Peter Charles L'Enfant, the French-born engineer who planned the new city, used the natural features of the land to their best advantage. For the site of the Capitol, he selected the western end of Jenkins Hill, which he described as "a pedestal waiting for a super-structure." In his plan, six important streets and avenues converged on the Capitol in a star pattern, and impressive views of the building would be available throughout the city.

L'Enfant would have designed the Capitol himself if President Washington hadn't fired him in February 1792. Instead, a competition was held to select a design. The winner was William Thornton, a physician and amateur architect. Thornton did not have the expertise to supervise the construction of the building, so that job was given to Stephen Hallet, who took second place in the competition. Ultimately, the Capitol was built following an amalgam of Thornton's exterior plan and Hallet's interior design.

George Washington set the cornerstone in a Masonic ceremony held on September 18, 1793. Work began on both the House and Senate wings, but only the Senate (north) wing was ready when Congress moved to Washington in 1800.

Hallet was fired in 1794, and responsibility for supervising the construction of the Capitol changed hands several times before the job was given to architect Benjamin Henry Latrobe in 1803. Latrobe finished the House wing in 1807, but the center section and dome would not be completed until more than two decades later. Instead, the two wings were connected by a covered wooden walkway.

On August 24, 1814, during the War of 1812, the British captured the city of Washington. That evening and the next day, they burned most of the public buildings in the city, including the Capitol. The wings of the unfinished building were largely gutted, and the exterior stonework was damaged. Latrobe set about rebuilding the wings, and they were almost finished at the time of his resignation in 1817.

Charles Bulfinch of Boston was soon appointed to fill Latrobe's position. Like each of his predecessors, Bulfinch altered the plans for the building to match his own tastes. He completed the Capitol using Latrobe's plans for the wings and east portico, but followed his own design for the west front, the rotunda (the circular room under the dome), and the low wooden dome. Work was completed in 1826, and the building retained this form until a new round of expansion began in 1851.

As new states were added to the Union, the number of legislators in Congress grew as well, and the Capitol was becoming increasingly cramped. While in 1800 there were 32 senators and 106 representatives, by 1850 the number had grown to 62 senators and 232 representatives (in 1911, the number of representatives was capped at 435). That same year, Congress appropriated funds for the building's expansion. A competition was held, and in 1851, Thomas U. Walter was selected as the architect. Walter's plan called for two new wings for the House and Senate, almost tripling the building's size. The cornerstone for the new wings was laid on July 4, 1851.

By 1855, it was apparent that Bulfinch's dome would be dwarfed by the newly expanded Capitol, and Congress authorized a replacement. Designed by Walter, the new dome was made of iron, painted white to match the rest of the building. It was a complex structure, with inner and outer domes supported by trusses, and was considered a great engineering marvel. Surmounting the dome was *Freedom*, a statue by Thomas Crawford. The statue's head was bolted in place on December 2, 1863, completing the dome.

Meanwhile, work continued on the wings. The House of Representatives held its first session in its new quarters in 1857, while the Senate first occupied its new wing in 1859. Work continued on the Capitol during the Civil War, when parts of the structure were used briefly as barracks for troops and as a hospital. By 1867, the wings were essentially finished, although the sculpture group decorating the east pediment of the House wing was not installed until 1916.

Between 1959 and 1961, the original east front, which appears in the photographs on this page, was extended outward 32½ feet. Before this modification, Walter's massive dome appeared ready to topple over the columned central portico. The extension corrected this illusion, while

The Capitol in its first stage of completion, c. 1846. It was built of Aquia sandstone painted white; the stone's natural color is a pale reddish gray. This daguerreotype is one of a small set by John Plumbe Jr.—the earliest known photographs of Washington, D.C.

adding offices and passageways that allow legislators to bypass the rotunda as they move through the building. The original east front was built of Aquia sandstone, a porous stone that withstood the weather poorly; the addition is a marble replica. The original sandstone walls are buried inside the structure; the columns were dismantled and later installed at the National Arboretum on New York Avenue, N.E.

The east front of the Capitol, c. 1905. The marble wings and iron dome were added between 1851 and 1867.

THE GROUNDS of the Capitol were laid out in the 1870s by Frederick Law Olmsted Sr., widely regarded as the father of American landscape architecture. Best known as the designer of Central Park in New York City, Olmsted finished the Capitol grounds in a similar manner, with winding paths and numerous trees arranged in a romantic, naturalistic manner. The grounds remain today essentially as he left them, and many of the trees have grown to impressive size.

In the first decades of the nineteenth century, the grounds of the Capitol were still largely wooded. Capitol Square, as it was then known, comprised only about 22 acres, less than half its present size. The first important improvements began under Charles Bulfinch, Architect of the Capitol from 1817 to 1829, who built a terrace on the west front following his own design. Bulfinch surrounded the grounds with an iron fence adorned with stone gateposts, installed two porter's lodges on the west, laid out paths, and planted trees and shrubs. In 1837, Congress extended Capitol Square westward to First Street, adding eight acres to the grounds.

In the 1850s, the Capitol was expanded with the addition of two wings. At that time, the grounds extended only to A Street North and A Street South, leaving each of the new wings only a few feet from the street! Congress did not remedy the situation until 1873, when it extended the grounds to their present limits at B Street North and B Street South (now Constitution and Independence avenues, respectively). That same year, Bulfinch's fence was relocated to the northern boundary of the Mall.

In 1874, Congress hired Frederick Law Olmsted Sr. to design landscaping for the grounds, which now comprised almost 60 acres. Olmsted started by clearing the square and removing a vast amount of fill, cutting down the hill to the west of the building. On the west side of the grounds, he replaced a dense stand of trees with a broad lawn, offering a magnificent view of the Capitol. He constructed a low stone wall around the perimeter, laid out paths, installed ornamental lanterns, and planted many trees and shrubs. The work was completed in 1881.

Olmsted's plan called for a new terrace on the west front of the Capitol. However, Congress was slow in providing funds, and work did not start until 1883. Olmsted's terrace has a high wall facing the Mall, lending the Capitol an appearance of greater height and stability (the existing terrace was faced with a high earthen embankment). It was completed in 1892.

In 2002, work began on the Capitol Visitor Center, which will accommodate the millions of tourists who come to the Capitol each year and provide improved security. Extending three levels below the East Plaza, it will feature two orientation theaters, a cafeteria, gift shops, exhibition space, and a grand staircase that will lead up into the Capitol. Besides the facilities for visitors, there will be office space and an auditorium for members of Congress and their staffs. The new visitor center is actually an immense underground building: The floor space comprises more than half a million square feet, two-thirds the size of the Capitol itself, and the cost is expected to exceed half a billion dollars. Completion is planned for 2008.

General Plan
for the
Improvement
OF THE
U. S. CAPITOL GROUNDS.

FRED. LAW OLMSTED
Landscape Architect

LEFT. The Peace Monument was the brainchild of Admiral David Dixon Porter, a naval commander in the Civil War and later superintendent of the U.S. Naval Academy. Porter selected the sculptor and supplied him with a rough sketch that was the basis for the monument's design.

RIGHT. Veterans of the Army of the Cumberland commissioned this memorial tribute to a fellow veteran, President James Garfield, shortly after his assassination. The statue's base was designed by Richard Morris Hunt, considered the father of Beaux-Arts architecture in America.

Erected in 1877, the Peace Monument stands in a small traffic circle at First Street and Pennsylvania Avenue. The work of sculptor Franklin Simmons, the monument is carved of white marble and rests on a base of blue granite. Known in the nineteenth century as the Naval Monument, it honors Union naval officers, seamen, and marines who died in the Civil War. The two allegorical figures atop the shaft represent America weeping on the shoulder of History. America mourns the naval personnel lost in the war, while History holds a book recording their heroic deeds. Facing the west (visible here) is a figure of Victory flanked by Neptune and Mars. On the opposite side is a female figure representing Peace.

The Garfield Memorial honors James A. Garfield (1831–1881), a Union general in the Civil War and president of the United States from March to September 1881. Dedicated in 1887, the memorial stands in a small traffic circle at First Street and Maryland Avenue. Garfield was shot on June 2, 1881, only a few blocks from here in the Baltimore and Potomac Railroad Station, and died 11 weeks later (see pages 80–81). The statue, sculpted by John Quincy Adams Ward, is made of bronze and rests on a marble base. Garfield appears to be giving a speech, while holding a sheaf of notes in his left hand. Three figures at the base represent Garfield's three careers as a scholar, a soldier, and a statesman.

The Ulysses S. Grant Memorial is the masterwork of sculptor Henry Merwin Shrady, who labored on it for almost 20 years, only to die shortly before its dedication in 1922. The memorial stands in front of the Capitol, symbolically facing the Lincoln Memorial at the opposite end of the Mall.

Congress passed legislation in 1901 that provided for a monument to Ulysses S. Grant (1822–1885), commander of the Union forces in the Civil War and president of the United States from 1869 to 1877. After a competition held the following year, the commission was awarded to Shrady, still a young man and relatively unknown as a sculptor.

Shrady's work features a bronze equestrian statue of Grant on a 252-foot-long marble base, flanked by four lions and two bronze equestrian groups, *Cavalry* and *Artillery*. The Grant statue depicts the general slouching in the saddle, with the wind at his back, stoic, as he was in war. The two equestrian groups are unmatched in their realism and drama: They evoke the chaos of war and the pain, excitement, and weariness of the troops simultaneously.

Shrady was a perfectionist, and his progress on the memorial was excruciatingly slow. High strung and in frail health, he spared no time or trouble in researching his subject. Shrady finished the lions first, and the base was installed in 1908 in what was then the Botanic Garden. Next, he sculpted the *Artillery Group* and the *Cavalry Group*, and, finally, completed the equestrian statue of Grant in 1919. Unfortunately, Shrady died only two weeks before his masterwork was dedicated on April 27, 1922. The two bronze panels on the pedestal of the Grant statue were finished by other artists.

The 1902 McMillan Plan suggested the memorial's present location. The surrounding area was to have been arranged as "Union Square," a great open space equal to the Place de la Concorde in Paris, but it was never fully realized. In the late 1960s, an interstate highway was constructed beneath the Mall in front of the Grant Memorial. The Capitol Reflecting Pool was constructed above the highway, but unfortunately, its wide expanse isolates the Grant Memorial from the Mall.

The Grant Memorial stands at the east end of the Mall, in the shadow of the Capitol. In the center, surrounded by four lions, is a statue of General Ulysses S. Grant, the second largest equestrian statue in the world. On the right is the *Artillery Group*, and on the left, hidden behind the Grant statue, is the *Cavalry Group*. Both depict Union troops in the Civil War.

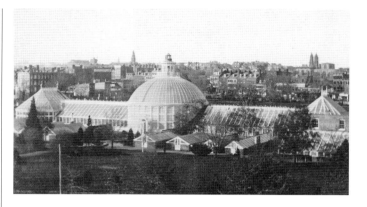

Housed in a newly renovated conservatory on Independence Avenue, the U.S. Botanic Garden is a museum of
living plants. There are approximately 4,000 individual
plants on public display at any one time. Highlights include the
Garden Primeval, a snapshot of plant life in the Jurassic Age, illustrated with primitive ferns and other living fossils; the Orchid
House, with hundreds of orchids, many in bloom; and the World
Desert, a display of cacti, succulents, and other desert plants. At the
center of the conservatory is the Jungle, a tropical rain forest growing amidst the faux ruins of a plantation.

The first botanic garden on the Mall was established by the
Columbian Institute for the Promotion of Arts and Sciences, a

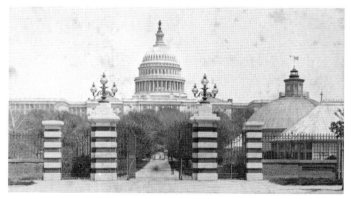

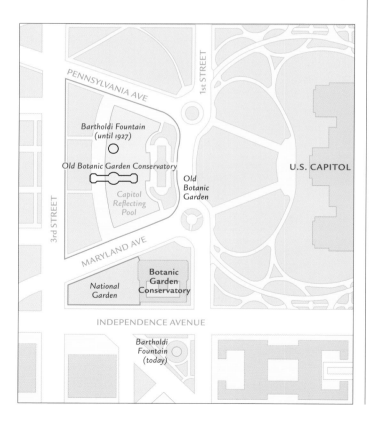

A plan of the U.S. Botanic Garden. Map labels: PENNSYLVANIA AVE, 1st STREET, 3rd STREET, MARYLAND AVE, Bartholdi Fountain (until 1927), Old Botanic Garden Conservatory, Capitol Reflecting Pool, Old Botanic Garden, U.S. CAPITOL, National Garden, Botanic Garden Conservatory, INDEPENDENCE AVENUE, Bartholdi Fountain (today)

private organization. Congress granted the institute use of a trapezoidal lot on the Mall (now the site of the Capitol Reflecting Pool) in 1820. The institute planted a modest garden where it propagated seeds and plants for distribution throughout the country. It also conducted lectures and held a collection of artifacts, including a military uniform that once belonged to George Washington (see page 71). The Columbian Institute and its garden disappeared around 1837.

The present U.S. Botanic Garden has its origins in the U.S. Exploring Expedition of 1838–1842, commanded by Lieutenant Charles Wilkes. Wilkes traveled around the world and returned with more than 250 live plants and thousands of plant specimens and seeds. The collections were placed under control of the Joint (Congressional) Committee on the Library, and in 1842, a greenhouse was built for them at the Patent Office, on F Street.

The Bartholdi Fountain in its original position on the grounds of the old Botanic Garden, now the site of the Capitol Reflecting Pool, in 1926. Frédéric Auguste Bartholdi, best known as the sculptor of the *Statue of Liberty*, designed the fountain for the 1876 Centennial Exhibition in Philadelphia. After the exhibition, the federal government bought the fountain and installed it at the Botanic Garden. It is made of painted cast iron and was equipped with gas lights, which were converted to electric ones. The fountain was removed in 1927 to make way for a monument to Civil War General George Gordon Meade (which was itself moved in 1967) and subsequently re-erected in a small triangular park south of Independence Avenue, now known as Bartholdi Park. These eight women are enacting a "tableau of peace and plenty" as part of a pageant honoring the International Council of Women.

In 1850, expansion of the Patent Office building forced the removal of the collections, and they were reinstalled on the Mall, on the same site that had been used by the Columbian Institute. To house the plants, a small octagonal conservatory was built that same year. It was intended to be the eastern pavilion of a much larger structure that could be completed later. Architect of the Capitol Edward Clark drew up plans for the enlarged building in 1867, and the work was finished by 1871. An important function of the garden was to introduce potentially useful foreign plants into the United States. It became a popular tourist attraction, as well, and supplied plants and cut flowers to members of Congress.

In the 1930s, following the 1902 McMillan Plan, the main axis of the Mall was cleared of trees and planted with a broad lawn bordered by symmetric rows of elm trees. The Botanic Garden, which straddled the centerline of the Mall, was demolished and rebuilt one block to the south, across Maryland Avenue. The architectural firm of Bennett, Parsons and Frost designed the conservatory in the Beaux-Arts style. It opened in 1933 and comprises a long narrow gallery on the north built of masonry faced with limestone and a 93-foot-high glass house on the south.

The glass house, considered innovative for its extensive use of aluminum, had deteriorated extensively by 1992, when the Architect of the Capitol demolished it as unsafe. The entire building closed from 1997 to 2001 for a renovation and was virtually rebuilt from the ground up.

Across Independence Avenue from the conservatory is Bartholdi Park, the location of the historic Bartholdi Fountain. The triangular park, created in 1932, now functions as a demonstration garden for home gardeners. To the west of the conservatory is the three-acre National Garden. Highlights include a rose garden, a water garden, and a display of plants native to the Mid-Atlantic region. Privately funded, the National Garden opened in 2006.

In his 1791 plan for the capital, Peter Charles L'Enfant included a canal that traversed the city, connecting the Potomac and Anacostia rivers. President George Washington, who closely supervised planning for the new federal city, was keenly interested in the canal for the role it would play in the development of the city as a commercial center. In an age before paved roads or railroads, the waterway was intended to speed goods to the city's markets.

In 1802, Congress incorporated the Washington Canal Company to build the canal following the course in L'Enfant's plan. Benjamin Henry Latrobe, a prominent architect and engineer, was hired to design it, but funds were insufficient, and the effort was a failure. Congress chartered a new company with the same name in 1809; work began the following year, and the canal opened in 1815.

The route of the Washington Canal can be seen on the Boschke map on page 13. The canal opened onto the Potomac River at Fifteenth Street, and followed B Street (now Constitution Avenue) east to Sixth Street, zigzagged across the Mall, then skirted Capitol Hill to the southwest, and joined the Anacostia River near the Navy Yard. The waterway served commerce for many years, but it was poorly maintained and often blocked with silt. Much of the city's sewage emptied into the canal, and it became an odorous, vile nuisance. In 1871, the city government began filling it in, starting east of Seventh Street. The work was completed the following year, and a sewer was constructed parallel to the canal bed under B Street.

In 1833 the Chesapeake and Ohio Canal was extended from Georgetown into Washington, linking it with the Washington Canal. The extension followed the shore through Foggy Bottom and opened to the Potomac at Seventeenth Street, where a lock was built. A small stone house, built there for the lockkeeper around 1835, has miraculously survived to the present day. The house originally stood on a narrow spit of land, with the Potomac only a few feet from its back door. In the late nineteenth century, the mud flats behind the house were filled, and the river is now more than one-half mile away! In the years since, the lockhouse has served as a tool shed, a public restroom, and a Park Police station. Today it is empty.

The Washington Canal on the Mall between Third and Sixth streets, 1858.

A view south across B Street (now Constitution Avenue), May 1902. The stone building still stands today. It was once a lockhouse on an extension of the Chesapeake and Ohio Canal, which opened to the Potomac at this spot. Within a year, Seventeenth Street was cut through the Mall just to the left of the building.

Tiber Creek once flowed along the north side of the Mall, but it has long since disappeared. From its headwaters near Florida Avenue, the creek ran south toward the Capitol, then turned and followed present-day Constitution Avenue, and emptied into the Potomac River south of the White House.

Where it flowed along the Mall, the Tiber (also known as Goose Creek) was slow moving and broad. It was 1,000 feet wide at its mouth and narrowed to about 200 feet at Seventh Street. Like the Potomac, its waters rose and fell with the tides. Christian Hines described the creek as it appeared in 1800:

There were ... a great many sycamore and other trees growing along the Tiber, the roots of which projected over the banks. I have often walked along, in company with others, in search of turtle nests.... On the south side there were fewer trees along the margin of the creek, and the embankment was much lower than on the north side [where it was as high as eight feet].... Large flocks of wild ducks could be seen on the Potomac. They would even come ... up the Tiber, at times, almost to where the Centre Market now stands. They would approach so near the shore that people used to throw stones at them.

In the early nineteenth century, the Washington Canal was built along the creek bed between Third and Fifteenth streets, and after that time, the creek emptied into the canal near the present-day Capitol Reflecting Pool (see the photograph on page 14). In 1872, the canal was filled in, and the Tiber was rerouted to the south. It flowed under the Mall through a sewer, into the James Creek Canal south of the Capitol, and to the Anacostia River. Over the years, the remainder of the Tiber was directed through sewers as well. The James Creek Canal, which appears on many early maps as a western leg of the Washington Canal, actually was begun as the latter canal was filled in. It survived until 1918.

Although the Tiber had been filled in, B Street (now Constitution Avenue) remained prone to flooding throughout the nineteenth century. The worst flood in the city's history was in 1889, when several feet of water covered Constitution Avenue, the eastern end of the Mall and Pennsylvania Avenue, and parts of the Federal Triangle. The flood was caused by heavy rains upstream, the same that precipitated the famous disaster at Johnstown, Pennsylvania.

In 1942, flood waters rose nearly as high as in 1889, but flooding in the city was much less severe. The reflecting pool was inundated, but a flood control berm in what is now Constitution Gardens prevented the water from reaching Constitution Avenue. A gap at Seventeenth Street, just south of the avenue, was blocked with sandbags. This precaution is still taken today when floodwaters threaten the city.

Tiber Creek flowing on the Mall near Third Street, 1868.

Missouri and Maine avenues were not part of Peter L'Enfant's original plan for the city. Rather, they were created in 1822 when the city government, acting under the authority of Congress, carved four city blocks out of the Mall and divided them into lots. Funds from the sale of the lots would compensate the city for the cost of moving a short section of the Washington Canal from Pennsylvania Avenue to the center of the Mall. It was hoped that the relocation of the canal would better drain the area around Third Street, which was then low and wet.

The two avenues were named for states that had recently been added to the union. Missouri Avenue ran between Third and Sixth streets on the north side of the Mall, while Maine Avenue was its mirror image on the south side (see the Boschke map on page 13). Missouri Avenue, located close to the heart of the city's commercial district, had a number of hotels, boarding houses, and fine private residences. One of these houses, at 467 Missouri Avenue, was the home of Vice President John Tyler for a brief period during in the 1840s.

The two blocks on Maine Avenue were altogether different. There were two foundries and a stoneyard, and a gas plant operated by the Washington Gas Light Company. Prior to 1947, homes and businesses in Washington burned *producer gas*, a flammable mixture of carbon monoxide and hydrogen. The gas was manufactured in plants, such as the one on the Mall, by heating coal or coke in the presence of steam.

A large house at 349 Maryland Avenue (the two blocks on Maine Avenue faced Maryland Avenue, as well) was home to a high-class brothel operated by Mary Ann Hall throughout the mid-nineteenth century. Archeologists investigated the site before the construction of the National Museum of the American Indian. They uncovered the foundations of the house and excavated a nearby trash pit, revealing many clues about the lifestyle of the women who lived and worked there. Cutting through the two blocks was Louse Alley (also known as Armory Place), which was lined with tiny rowhouses where poverty-stricken residents lived in cramped and unsanitary conditions. Such inhabited alleys, found throughout the city, were notorious as breeding grounds for disease and vice.

In the 1930s, the National Park Service acquired Missouri and Maine avenues and the four adjacent blocks. Following the recommendations of the 1902 McMillan Commission, which hoped to return the Mall to the intentions of Peter L'Enfant, the Park Service cleared the buildings and restored the original 1,600-foot width of the Mall between Constitution and Independence avenues. Missouri and Maine avenues were eliminated, and their names were reassigned to streets elsewhere in the city.

LEFT. Looking northwest at the intersection of Missouri Avenue (left) and Third Street, c. 1930. Missouri Avenue was soon closed, and the buildings were demolished. It is now the site of the East Building of the National Gallery of Art.

RIGHT. Looking east on Maine Avenue from the old Washington Armory, April 1865. These blocks were cleared in the 1930s as part of a broad program for the improvement of the Mall.

A 1915 rendering shows the George Washington Memorial building as it would have appeared from the Mall, had it been completed.

The George Washington Memorial building would have stood on Constitution Avenue, on the site of the present-day National Gallery of Art, as a monument to the first president. The cornerstone was laid in 1921, but work never advanced beyond the foundations, since the private association sponsoring the project was unable to raise the necessary funds. The white marble edifice would have had a 300-foot-long façade facing the Mall ornamented with 16 Ionic columns, 48 feet high. Inside there would have been an auditorium seating at least 6,000 persons; other smaller assembly rooms; 58 rooms for each state and territory to be used for exhibits; and offices for "patriotic, scientific, educational, and other organizations of national scope." The building would have served as a convention center as well, a facility then lacking in Washington.

The memorial building was sponsored by the George Washington Memorial Association, formed in 1897 specifically for this purpose. Congress granted the association the Mall site in 1913. Prominent architects Evarts Tracy and Egerton Swartwout of New York designed the building, but the association was only able to raise a fraction of the cost. After World War I, the association changed the name of the building to the George Washington *Victory* Memorial. It proposed covering the domed ceiling of the building's great auditorium with 5 million stars, blue for those who served in the war, and gold for those who died. Each star would bear a name, which could be read from the floor below with the aid of a telescope. Each state would pay for the stars representing its own sons and daughters, and in this way, the building's construction costs would be covered.

President Warren G. Harding delivered the principal address at the cornerstone setting ceremony on November 14, 1921. Work did not actually begin until 1923, however. The foundations were soon completed, but for lack of funds, the superstructure was never begun. The foundations remained exposed for more than a decade, until they were removed in 1937, as the site was cleared for the National Gallery of Art. The George Washington Memorial Association dissolved itself the following year.

Men chop wood in the unfinished foundation of the building as part of a Depression-era make-work project, August 1935.

Paul Mellon and his father, Andrew W. Mellon. The elder Mellon founded the National Gallery of Art. Paul and his sister Ailsa donated funds for the East Building and gave a dazzling array of artworks.

RIGHT. The West Building of the National Gallery of Art, seen from the Mall. The East Building is visible at the far right.

The National Gallery of Art, on the north side of the Mall between Third and Seventh streets, opened in 1941, a gift to the nation from Andrew W. Mellon. The gallery has a superb collection of European and American art dating from the late Middle Ages to the present. Highlights include more than a dozen paintings by Rembrandt van Rijn and the only painting by Leonardo da Vinci in the Western Hemisphere.

Andrew W. Mellon (1855–1937) was born in Pittsburgh and lived there most of his life. A banker and financier, he helped found the Aluminum Company of America (Alcoa), Gulf Oil Company, and the Union Steel Company. Perhaps the third richest man in America, he was largely unknown to the public before becoming secretary of the treasury in 1921. He served for 11 years under Republican presidents Harding, Coolidge, and Hoover. Mellon was wildly popular in the post, as the 1920s were a time of great prosperity. With the onset of the Great Depression, however, his popularity faded, and President Hoover appointed him ambassador to Britain in 1932, a position he held until Franklin Roosevelt became president the following year.

Mellon began collecting art as a young man, but it was during his tenure as secretary of the treasury that he developed his idea to found a national gallery, an ambition that he concealed as best he could. Mellon began to assemble a collection of masterpieces of the highest quality to form the core of the future gallery's collection. His most spectacular acquisition was a group of 21 paintings from the Hermitage Museum in Leningrad, bought in 1930 and 1931 from the Soviet government, which was in desperate need of hard currency. The group included Raphael's *Alba Madonna*, the first work of art to be sold for $1 million; five paintings by Rembrandt; and works by Botticelli, van Dyck, Titian, and others.

Mellon even selected the site for the gallery and hired its architect, John Russell Pope. The gallery was already a well-developed concept when he offered the building and his collection to the United States in December 1936. Mellon was now in poor health and the target of a politically motivated prosecution for tax evasion by the Roosevelt administration. He could have taken his gift elsewhere, but believed in the importance of having a national gallery in Washington.

In March 1937, Congress passed legislation that accepted Mellon's gift and established the National Gallery of Art. The gallery is technically an independent bureau of the Smithsonian Institution, but it is part of the Smithsonian in name only. Congress pledged the faith of the United States to pay for the gallery's operation. Mellon paid for the building, which cost $15 million, and donated 142 works of art, the core of the collection. It was said to be the largest gift ever made by an individual to a government.

Architect John Russell Pope was a classicist in the Beaux-Arts tradition, a style that enjoyed its heyday at the turn of the century, but had largely passed out of fashion by 1937. The central portion of the building, with a dome and porticos, is based on the Pantheon in Rome. True to Beaux-Arts principles, the building has strong axial relationships: Its plan takes the form of a cross, like the Mall itself. Work began in 1937. The building was constructed of steel and masonry, faced with

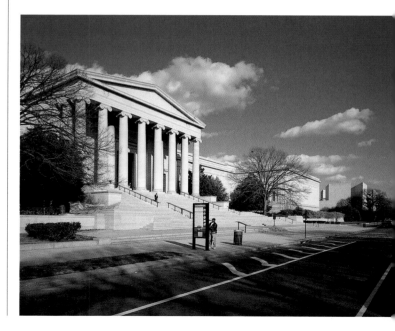

blocks of pink Tennessee marble. The darkest stone was placed at the base of the structure, with the color graduating toward the top. At 782 feet in length, the building is longer than the U.S. Capitol.

Mellon died in August 1937. To encourage gifts by other collectors, he had stipulated that the National Gallery not carry his name, a tactic that was evidently successful. Even before the gallery opened, Samuel H. Kress, founder of a chain of dime stores, had donated his collection of Italian art. At the time, it was considered the best in the world in private hands. The building was completed in December 1940, and the National Gallery was dedicated on March 17, 1941. In its early years, the museum built its collection with major gifts from Joseph Widener, Lessing J. Rosenwald, the Mellon family, Chester Dale, and others.

By 1967, the gallery had become quite cramped. That year, Paul Mellon, Andrew Mellon's son, and his sister, Ailsa Mellon Bruce, offered to fund the construction of a new gallery building on a site just to the east of the original building. For the awkwardly shaped site, architect I. M. Pei designed a trapezoidal building that comprised two triangular structures, one housing exhibition space and the other housing offices, a library, and storage space for drawings and prints.

Work on the new East Building began in 1971. It was built of cast concrete faced with the same pink Tennessee marble used for the West Building (as the original building is known today). The East Building is essentially modern in style. The enormous atrium, with balconies, escalators, and a bridge, was designed to foster a sense of excitement in visitors. The galleries were built on a small scale so that the art could be seen in an intimate setting. The East Building opened to the public in 1978. Although it was projected to cost $20 million, the Mellon family eventually gave almost $100 million for its construction.

The National Sculpture Garden is located west of the West Building, directly across the Mall from the Hirshhorn Museum's sculpture garden. It opened in 1999 and contains a fine collection of modern and contemporary sculpture scattered along winding paths. The landscaping, designed by landscape architect Laurie D. Olin of Philadelphia, is laid out in a naturalistic manner.

A sculpture garden had been planned for the site since the 1960s. A skating rink opened there in 1974, and a pavilion was completed in 1988. The garden was finally constructed between 1997 and 1999, largely funded by a gift of $10 million from the Morris and Gwendolyn Cafritz Foundation. The 1974 rink was replaced with a fountain that serves as a rink in the winter months. The pavilion and many of the existing trees were preserved during the construction of the new garden.

James Smithson (1765–1829), an English scientist who had never seen the United States, bequeathed his fortune to found the Smithsonian Institution.

Joseph Henry (1797–1878) was a prominent physicist and the Smithsonian's first secretary.

TOP RIGHT. The Smithsonian Institution building, or the Castle, in an 1862 photograph. Begun in 1847, it was the first of many Smithsonian buildings on the Mall.

The Smithsonian Institution was established in 1846 with a bequest from James Smithson, an English scientist. Today, it comprises 10 museums on the Mall, the largest museum complex in the world. The Smithsonian functions as the "nation's attic," preserving and displaying untold millions of objects related to history, culture, science, technology, and art. The institution also operates the National Zoo in Northwest Washington, several museums off the Mall, and research facilities around the world.

James Smithson was born in 1765 in France, the illegitimate son of Elizabeth Keate Macie and Hugh Smithson (who later became the first Duke of Northumberland). Due to the circumstances of his birth, Smithson was unable to inherit his father's titles and property and was barred from many public positions. Instead, he pursued a career on the continent as a scientist, supported by a large inheritance from his mother's family. Smithson associated with some of the greatest minds of the day and published dozens of papers on chemistry and mineralogy.

Smithson died in 1829, leaving his fortune to a nephew. His will stipulated that if the nephew were to die without heirs, his legacy would go to the "united states of america, to found at Washington, under the name to the Smithsonian institution, an establishment for the increase & diffusion of Knowledge among men." Smithson probably hoped to bring immortality to his name, something that had eluded him as a scientist. But why the United States, a country he had never visited? He no doubt resented the limitations of his birth, and as an anti-royalist and a product of the Age of Enlightenment, he might have believed that the American republic represented a greater hope for mankind than did his native Britain.

Smithson's nephew died without heirs six years later, and in 1836, Congress accepted the bequest. Smithson's gift, gold sovereigns worth £100,000, was brought to the United States and reminted as American coin. Congress took almost a decade to decide what form the "establishment for the increase & diffusion of Knowledge" should take. Various congressmen supported a library, an observatory, a lecture bureau, and schools of various sorts. After lengthy debate, Congress passed an act in 1846 establishing the Smithsonian Institution,

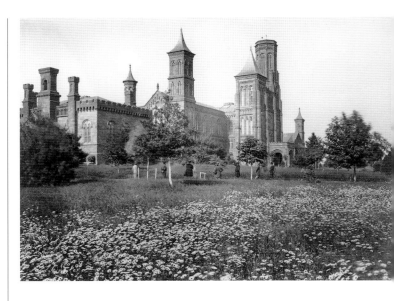

specifying that it combine a laboratory, a library, an art gallery, and space for natural history collections and public lectures. The institution would be directed by a board of regents and supported by the interest on the principal of Smithson's bequest.

The act specified that the institution have a building, and the board of regents promptly selected a site on the Mall. They held a design competition, which they awarded to James Renwick Jr., of New York. Although only in his 20s, Renwick was already a prominent architect. Stylistically, his building (see the photograph above) is an early example of Medieval Revival. It is romantic and picturesque, with an asymmetric layout and rusticated red sandstone surfaces. There are eight towers, each different in size, form, and detail. Robert Dale Owen, a congressman and member of the board of regents, saw the building as a prototype for a native American architectural style, but this never came to pass. The cornerstone was laid in 1847, and the building opened to the public in 1855.

In 1846, the board of regents selected Joseph Henry as the first secretary of the Smithsonian Institution. Henry was a nationally prominent scientist, a pioneer in the study of electromagnetism, and a professor at the College of New Jersey (today's Princeton University). In spite of the broad congressional mandate, Henry believed that the Smithsonian should be dedicated to scientific research and resisted pressures to support a library or other activities as an unnecessary drain on the institution's scarce resources. In 1850, Henry hired Spencer Fullerton Baird as assistant secretary (he would succeed Henry in 1878). Baird was a naturalist and, unlike Henry, an avid collector. He was influential in building the Smithsonian's collections and developing the institution as a museum.

Because of its small budget, the Smithsonian had less effect on the progress of science than Henry might have wished, but it quickly accumulated the best natural history collections in the nation. The institution had representatives on dozens of government exploratory expeditions in the American West and overseas who sent back specimens, and amateurs also contributed. At the Smithsonian, there was a staff of scientists, including botanists, naturalists, and others, who classified specimens in the labs and ventured into the field as well. The institution also supported a number of ethnologists, who gathered data on the vanishing culture of the American Indians.

Before the Civil War, the Castle held a large display of natural history specimens in the Great Hall on the ground floor. The second floor housed an art gallery with hundreds of portraits of American Indians by John Mix Stanley and Charles Bird King. In January 1865, a fire destroyed the upper floor and the three central towers. The Indian portraits (those by Stanley represented the bulk of his life's work) were destroyed, along with James Smithson's personal papers and many other items.

The Smithsonian sponsored a large display at the 1876 Centennial Exhibition in Philadelphia. Afterward, Baird secured many additional exhibits from the exhibition for the institution. These were shipped to Washington by train and stored on the Mall in the old armory. Congress soon appropriated money for a new building to display the material, and work started in 1879 on a site just east of the Castle. Known as the National Museum (today, it is the Arts and Industries building), it followed the design of Washington architects Adolph Cluss and Paul Shulze and was completed in

Top. Museum exhibits in the Castle's Great Hall, 1867. Today, the hall is an information center for visitors.

Bottom. Bison in a corral in the South Yard of the Castle, c. 1888. The bison were among a number of animals that were used as taxidermy models by William T. Hornaday, curator of living animals. The collection became the core of the National Zoological Park when it was established in 1889, with Hornaday as its first superintendent. The zoo was established at the initiative of Hornaday, who feared that the bison would soon be extinct and hoped that the zoo might aid in their preservation. Today, the National Zoological Park has about 2,800 animals at its 163-acre site on Connecticut Avenue in Northwest Washington. It is still part of the Smithsonian Institution.

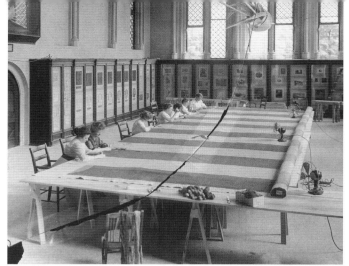

1881. Similar to a building at the Centennial Exhibition, and influenced by exhibition buildings in Europe, the Arts and Industries building is an eclectic mix of Romanesque and Renaissance elements. It was built of brick with a lightweight iron-and-glass roof, and polychrome brick decorates the exterior.

The old National Museum building held much more than relics from the Centennial Exhibition. On display was a vast collection of objects representing natural history, ethnology, industry, and American history. There were exhibits in the Castle as well. Birds, shells, corals, and sponges were on the ground floor; archeology was on the

National Museum, Washington

second. George Brown Goode, in charge of the National Museum in the late nineteenth century, was a pioneer in exhibit design. At that time, exhibits were often arrays of nearly identical objects that could be appreciated only by an expert. Goode believed that a careful selection of representative items, each with an educational label, would better serve visitors.

The natural history exhibits were moved to the new National Museum (today's Natural History building) in 1910, and for the next half century, the Arts and Industries building would be jammed with objects related to history, technology, and aviation, such as the Star-Spangled Banner and the Wright brothers' *Flyer*. These exhibits were, in turn, relocated in the 1960s and '70s when the American History and Air and Space museums were completed.

In 1976, "1876: A Centennial Exhibition" opened in the Arts and Industries building to mark the nation's bicentennial, with displays similar to those at the 1876 exhibition in Philadelphia. The last portion of this exhibit was removed in 1999, and the building subsequently closed, awaiting renovation.

During most of the twentieth century, the west wing of the Smithsonian Castle showcased prints and printing technology. Today, the Great Hall, on the ground floor, is home to the Smithsonian Information Center, where visitors can learn about the Smithsonian's many museums.

TOP LEFT. Charles Lindbergh's plane, the Ryan NYP *Spirit of Saint Louis*, hangs from the ceiling of the Arts and Industries building, c. 1930. Lindbergh flew the plane on the first solo, nonstop flight across the Atlantic in 1927. The following year, he donated it to the Smithsonian.

TOP RIGHT. Natural history exhibits on display in the Arts and Industries building, c. 1930.

In 1953, Leonard Carmichael was appointed the seventh secretary of the Smithsonian, ushering in a period of dramatic change. Carmichael hoped to expand and modernize the institution, then stagnant and underfunded. Charming, urbane, and politically sophisticated, he had the skills to get the necessary money from Congress. During his 10 years as secretary, the Smithsonian's appropriations increased more than fivefold. At the same time, the Smithsonian built the American History Museum, acquired the old Patent Office downtown, expanded the Natural History Museum and modernized its exhibits, and started planning for the new National Air Museum.

The Smithsonian's great expansion continued under the eighth secretary, S. Dillon Ripley, who served from 1964 to 1984. Besides improving the Smithsonian's financial resources and its facilities, Ripley was interested in attracting a larger audience. In 1967, he opened the Anacostia Neighborhood Museum, installed a carousel on the Mall, and started the Festival of American Folklife (now the Smithsonian Folklife Festival), an annual event. The National Air and Space Museum was completed in 1976, and it soon became the most popular museum in the world.

Ripley expanded the Smithsonian's art holdings dramatically, opening the National Portrait Gallery and the Smithsonian American Art Museum in downtown Washington, as well as the Renwick Gallery near the White House. He acquired Joseph Hirshhorn's collection of modern art and installed it in a museum on the Mall and began the Quadrangle Project, with two art museums: the Sackler Gallery and the National Museum of African Art.

The Smithsonian's newest museum on the Mall is the National Museum of the American Indian, which opened in 2004. Located on an odd-shaped lot east of the Air and Space Museum, it accommodates a superb collection of American Indian artifacts acquired in 1989 when the private Museum of the American Indian in New York City was absorbed by the Smithsonian.

The Smithsonian Castle was built of red sandstone from Seneca, Maryland, just up the Potomac River from Washington. On the south side of the building is the Enid A. Haupt Garden, which opened in 1987.

The National Museum of Natural History opened to the public in 1910. Until 1957, it was known simply as the National Museum.

ATTRACTIONS such as the Hope diamond, a collection of fossil dinosaur bones, an IMAX theater, and an insect zoo draw hordes of visitors to the National Museum of Natural History every year. Indeed, it is the second-most-visited museum in the world, surpassed only by the National Air and Space Museum.

The museum was constructed between 1904 and 1911 to house the Smithsonian's ever-expanding natural history collections. It was originally called the *new* National Museum to distinguish it from the *old* National Museum, as the Arts and Industries building was known. The building was Beaux-Arts in design, the work of the architectural firm of Hornblower and Marshall of Washington and was the first on the Mall to conform to the 1902 McMillan Plan. It was constructed of steel and brick and faced with blocks of white granite.

Although the museum was built to display natural history specimens, it featured other exhibits as well. The Smithsonian art collections were displayed in the building from its opening in March 1910 until the 1960s. In the 1920s, the War Collection, a group of military relics from World War I, was displayed on the ground floor and in the rotunda, and in the 1930s there was a large exhibition of lace on the second floor.

A century ago, museum employees pioneered exhibition techniques that are commonplace today. William Henry Holmes introduced the ethnological group, full-sized figures arranged in a tableau of everyday life, and William T. Hornaday was among the first to mount animals in a natural setting. Then as now, museum employees were primarily engaged in research and in building and maintaining the collections of natural history specimens. When times were lean, as they often were, there was little money to spare for developing new exhibits.

In the late 1950s and early 1960s, exhibits throughout the museum were modernized. The standalone mahogany cases dating from the 1910s and 1920s were replaced with cases set into the walls. Many of these exhibits, now more than 40 years old, are still in place. Further modernization of the museum's permanent exhibits is underway.

Two wings were added to the building between 1961 and 1964 to provide additional space for offices, laboratories, and storage. In 1999, the Discovery Center, an essentially freestanding building constructed in the west courtyard, opened to the public. It features a 487-seat IMAX theater, a new restaurant, and a museum shop. A similar building in the east courtyard holds additional office space.

LEFT. Preparing the skeleton of a juvenile dinosaur for exhibition at the National Museum, 1921.

RIGHT. Art was displayed at the Natural History Museum until the 1960s. These sculptures in the rotunda were part of a 1932 exhibit marking the bicentennial of George Washington's birth.

THE NATIONAL MUSEUM of American History was the first Smithsonian museum to be built in the period of great expansion that began in the late 1950s under Secretary Leonard Carmichael. Opening to the public in January 1964 as the Museum of History and Technology, it was intended to demonstrate the progress of the American people since the colonial period in every realm, but especially in technology.

Many of the objects in the new museum were transferred from the perennially crowded Arts and Industries building. For instance, the exhibit "First Ladies: Political Role and Public Image," a collection of gowns that once belonged to presidents' wives, was first displayed in the Arts and Industries building about 1915. Today, the National Museum of American History is the guardian of some of America's greatest historical icons, such as the Star-Spangled Banner, which inspired the United States' national anthem. Other highlights include Horatio Greenough's statue of Washington (see page 54) and the 1831 *John Bull* steam locomotive, the oldest functional locomotive in the world.

Ground was broken for the new museum in 1958, and construction began the following year, paid for with a large appropriation from Congress. The architect was James Kellum Smith of the firm McKim, Mead and White. (Smith died before work was completed

and was replaced by Walker O. Cain.) The architects attempted a modern reinterpretation of a classical colonnade, but the result was poorly received by architectural critics.

If the exterior was dull and uninspiring, the interior was considered innovative, with its large, flexible exhibition spaces. Contemporary writers made much of the escalators and extra drinking fountains mounted low for children, concessions to the comfort of visitors. Since 1980, the museum has been known as the National Museum of American History.

In 2000, a new permanent exhibition, "The American Presidency: A Glorious Burden," opened on the third floor. It illustrates the history of the American presidency with 900 artifacts, including George Washington's military uniform and sword, and the hat worn by Abraham Lincoln on the night of his assassination. New transportation and military history exhibits soon followed. In 2006, the museum closed for renovations that will include a new display area for the Star-Spangled Banner. A dramatic three-story atrium will be constructed at the Mall entrance, and the building's electrical and mechanical systems will be replaced. The work will be paid for in part with a gift of $80 million from Kenneth E. Behring, a California real estate developer.

TOP. This military uniform, on display at the American History Museum, once belonged to George Washington. It was most likely made in the 1780s, after Washington resigned from the Continental Army and before he became president. In 1828, Thomas Law, a friend of Washington's, gave the uniform to the Columbian Institute (see page 59). The uniform was transferred around 1840 to the National Institute, an early scientific society, and in 1883 to the Smithsonian.

LEFT. The National Museum of American History opened to the public in 1964. There are three levels of exhibit space. The lowest level extends below the terrace in the foreground.

Top. The National Air and Space Museum seen from the Mall. The three north-facing glass bays provide indirect sunlight for the exhibits.

Bottom left. The Aircraft building was constructed during World War I for the testing of aircraft engines. After the war, it housed the Smithsonian's aeronautical exhibits. The building stood in the South Yard of the Castle, on Independence Avenue, which appears on the left in this 1930s photograph. It was demolished in 1975, after the exhibits were transferred to the new National Air and Space Museum.

Bottom right. A Fokker D.VII biplane on display in the old Aircraft building. The plane was captured intact in the last days of World War I when its German pilot mistakenly landed on an American-controlled airfield. It is currently on display in the National Air and Space Museum.

Reflecting America's domination of aviation's first century, the National Air and Space Museum has the world's most comprehensive collection of objects related to aviation and space exploration. The treasures on display include the Wright brothers' 1903 *Flyer*, the world's first successful airplane; the Bell x-1, in which Captain Charles E. "Chuck" Yeager was the first to break the sound barrier, in 1947; and the Apollo 11 command module *Columbia*, used in the first mission to put astronauts on the moon.

For more than a half century, the Smithsonian's aeronautical collections were displayed in the Aircraft building, which stood in the South Yard of the Castle, along Independence Avenue. The exhibits included airplanes, engines, propellers, and models of various aircraft. Airplanes were displayed in the Arts and Industries building, as well, where some were hung by cables from the ceiling.

The National Air Museum was created as a bureau of the Smithsonian in 1946, but it would be three decades before the collections had their own building. The site between Fourth and Seventh streets was selected in 1958, and in 1966, Congress authorized a new building to be called the National Air and Space Museum. A design by architect Gyo Obata of Helmuth, Obata and Kassabaum was approved but not funded because of the Vietnam War. When interest in the project revived in 1970, the $40 million budget was no longer adequate, and the building had to be completely redesigned to lower its cost. A groundbreaking ceremony was held in 1972, and the new museum was dedicated on July 1, 1976, by President Gerald Ford.

The building was designed to provide maximum volume on a long narrow lot. Facing the Mall, open glass bays alternate with cubes made of thin marble panels mounted on a steel frame; the structure of the building is made of steel. The stone is pink Tennessee marble of the same variety used in the National Gallery of Art across the Mall. In the interior, aircraft are suspended, where they can be seen against the sky.

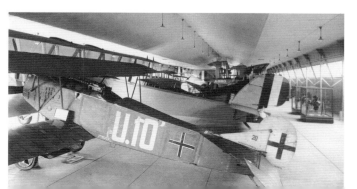

OPENED TO THE PUBLIC IN 1974, the Hirshhorn Museum and Sculpture Garden is dedicated to modern and contemporary art. The Hirshhorn holds some 12,000 works, including one of the best collections of modern sculpture in the world. About 600 objects are on display at any one time.

The core of the collection, about 6,000 works of modern art, was the gift of Joseph H. Hirshhorn (1899–1981), a Latvian-born financier. Actively pursued by Smithsonian Secretary S. Dillon Ripley, Hirshhorn agreed in 1966 to give his collection to the institution. The building was paid for almost entirely by the federal government, which is also responsible for operating expenses. Special exhibitions and additions to the collection are largely funded by donations.

Ground was broken for the museum in 1969. Gordon Bunshaft of Skidmore, Owings and Merrill was the architect. The building is an immense drum, 231 feet in diameter and 82 feet high, supported by four piers. It is appropriately modern in style, although some critics have likened its appearance to that of a gun turret.

The exterior, originally intended to be covered in pink travertine limestone, was instead made of concrete to lower costs. On the inside, the circular layout of the floors makes navigating the museum easy for visitors. The permanent collection is displayed principally on the third floor. Temporary exhibitions can be found on the second floor, while contemporary (i.e., recent and experimental) art is on the lower level.

The original plan for the outdoor sculpture garden was a 14-foot-deep trench that would have stretched across the Mall, effectively severing it in two. It was built following a less-obtrusive design because of public outcry, but it was still criticized as harsh and brutally unsympathetic to the art it contained. Stark and modernist, the "garden" was in reality a gravel-lined pit. A 1981 renovation added trees and grass, humanizing the space. In 1993, the square plaza around the building received a similar treatment.

The Hirshhorn Museum and Sculpture Garden has one of the world's best collections of modern sculpture. In the foreground is Joan Miró's bronze *Lunar Bird*. To the right is Mark di Suvero's red painted steel *Are Years What? (for Marianne Moore)*, acquired by the museum in 1999.

*The Burghers of Calais*, 1884–1889, is one of 12 casts of Auguste Rodin's masterpiece.

The Freer Gallery of Art, as it appeared shortly after its opening in 1923.

Housing a rare collection of Asian art and American paintings of the aesthetic movement, the Freer Gallery, which opened in 1923, was the first museum on the Mall dedicated exclusively to art. The gallery building and its collections were the gift of Charles Lang Freer, a Detroit industrialist who built a fortune manufacturing railcars.

Freer, born in 1854, retired while still a relatively young man and devoted himself to the study and collection of Asian art, at a time when few other Western collectors were interested. Asia was passing through a period of instability, and with his considerable financial resources and discriminating eye, Freer amassed a collection of extraordinary quality. He also patronized a select group of American painters, especially James McNeill Whistler. Freer considered Whistler the greatest artist of the nineteenth century, and today the museum has the most comprehensive collection of Whistler's work in the world.

After giving his collection to the Smithsonian in 1906 (it remained at Freer's home in Detroit until after his death), Freer dedicated his life to improving it, and it grew from about 2,000 objects to 11,000 at the time of his death in 1919. Freer placed several onerous restrictions on the gallery: It could neither lend nor borrow objects and could accept gifts from only a few individuals, whom Freer named. Additions of any sort to the American collection were prohibited.

Freer personally selected the gallery's architect, Charles Adams Platt. Platt's design conformed to the 1902 McMillan Plan: It was classically inspired, built of gray granite, and properly set back from the center of the Mall. The building is in the form of an Italian Renaissance palace.

It has one aboveground floor, a half basement, and a square courtyard.

Perhaps the best known and most popular exhibit in the Freer is the "Peacock Room." The room was originally in the London home of Frederick R. Leyland. James McNeill Whistler decorated the room to harmonize with his painting *The Princess from the Land of Porcelain,* and Leyland displayed his collection of blue and white porcelain there. In 1904 Freer bought the room and installed it in his Detroit mansion. He later bequeathed it to the Freer Gallery.

In 1988, the Freer closed for renovations lasting more than four years, at which time it was joined by a tunnel to the subterranean Sackler Gallery. Today the two museums are essentially one and the same, sharing the same staff, director, and many of the same facilities. The Sackler is not bound by the restrictions of Freer's bequest and can welcome visiting exhibitions and lend objects to other museums. In addition, the renovations sought to make the Freer more inviting to visitors; in spite of its extraordinary collections, it is one of the least-visited museums on the Mall.

Right. The "Peacock Room" in the Freer Gallery of Art. Over the fireplace hangs James McNeill Whistler's *The Princess from the Land of Porcelain.* Whistler decorated the room to harmonize with the painting.

THE NATIONAL MUSEUM of African Art has a collection of 8,000 works of art from Africa, dating from antiquity to the present day, of which about 300 are on display at any one time. It shares an underground building with the Arthur M. Sackler Gallery, a museum of Asian art. Only the entrance pavilions of the two museums appear above the surface; the remaining 96 percent is below ground level.

The African Art Museum was established as an independent museum in 1964 by Warren Robbins, an American diplomat and art collector. It was originally located on Capitol Hill, in the former home of abolitionist Frederick Douglass and some adjacent rowhouses. Over the years, the museum grew, and in 1979, it merged with the Smithsonian Institution.

In the early 1980s, the Smithsonian was under pressure from Congress to move the African Art Museum to the Mall. At the same time, it acquired a collection of Asian art from Arthur M. Sackler, a physician and medical publisher, along with $4 million for the construction of a gallery. By that time, aboveground space on the Mall was in short supply, leading to a decision to build the two museums underground in the Quadrangle behind the Smithsonian Castle.

In 1983, ground was broken for the Quadrangle complex, as the subterranean building is known. The architect was Jean Paul Carlhian of the architectural firm Shepley Bulfinch Richardson and Abbott of Boston. The structure extends 60 feet below the surface, 24 feet below the watertable, requiring elaborate waterproofing. The two museums occupy the first two levels below grade and part of the third. Also on the third level is the S. Dillon Ripley Center, with space for exhibits, offices, and public programs.

The Arthur M. Sackler Gallery opened in the new building in 1987. The Sackler collection, with 1,000 works of Asian art, formed the core of its collection. Two other notable acquisitions have been the Vever collection of Islamic manuscripts, and the Singer collection, a 5,000-object trove of ancient Chinese art.

The Enid A. Haupt Garden, located in the Quadrangle above the two museums, was completed in 1987. It was established with a gift of $3 million from Enid Annenberg Haupt, a sister of publisher and philanthropist Walter Annenberg. The carriage gates on the south side of the Quadrangle were built in 1979, following plans drawn in the nineteenth century by James Renwick Jr., architect of the Smithsonian Castle.

The Sackler Gallery and the African Art Museum share an underground building beneath the Enid A. Haupt Garden. On the left, in the foreground, is the gray granite entrance pavilion of the Sackler Gallery; on the right is the pink granite entrance pavilion of the African Art museum. The two museums opened in 1987.

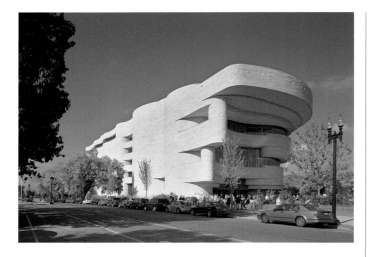

The National Museum of the American Indian opened on the Mall in 2004. This is the main entrance, at Third Street and Maryland Avenue.

THE NATIONAL MUSEUM of the American Indian, which opened in 2004, is positioned between the National Air and Space Museum and the Botanic Garden, taking what was widely considered the last available site on the Mall. Rather than treating native peoples as a historical curiosity whose time has passed, the new museum allows contemporary American Indians to tell their own story. The message is that native peoples are alive and well; having survived many trials, they are remarkably diverse, yet retain their own distinctive identity. The museum boasts a collection of American Indian art and artifacts that is considered by many to be the best in the world, but only a tiny fraction of it is on display. Rather, the focus is on contemporary native communities, and the artifacts play a supporting role.

The core collection was amassed in the early twentieth century by George Gustav Heye (1874–1957), an investment banker and heir to an oil fortune. An omnivorous collector, Heye spent five decades traveling throughout the Americas and Europe, purchasing every native object in sight. To share his treasures with the public, Heye opened a museum in New York's then-fashionable Washington Heights, at Broadway and 155th Street, in 1922. By the 1980s, however, the area had become a dangerous slum, and the priceless artifacts were stored in appalling conditions in the cramped, sparsely attended museum.

After lengthy negotiations, the Smithsonian Institution acquired the 800,000-object collection in 1989. It became the core of the National Museum of the American Indian, which was created by an act of Congress that same year. Following the terms of the agreement, the Heye collection would retain its own identity, remaining separate from other Smithsonian museums. In 1994, a branch museum opened in the U.S. Custom House in lower Manhattan, fulfilling a requirement of the acquisition agreement that the museum retain a presence in New York. Construction of the Mall museum building began in September 1999.

Architect Douglas Cardinal of Canada, himself an Indian of mixed blood, was hired in 1993 to design the Mall museum in association with GBQC Architects of Philadelphia. Cardinal already had an international reputation as an architect. His best-known work, the Canadian Museum of Civilization in Hull, Quebec, is considered one of the most architecturally important buildings in Canada. Furthermore, his organic, curvilinear style was considered appropriate for the American Indian Museum.

Cardinal left the project in 1998 after a bitter dispute with the Smithsonian over provisions of his contract, but by that time, he had worked out the essentials of his design. The work was completed by another architectural team, and the museum's exterior has been well received by critics.

Cardinal's challenge was to design a building that would be a powerful assertion of Native American identity, while looking at home on the classically ordered Mall. The resulting structure appears as an abstracted version of a natural rock outcrop. The exterior is clad in Kasota dolomitic limestone from Minnesota, arranged in layers that give the appearance of naturally stratified and eroded stone. On the east, facing the Capitol, is the main entrance, a dramatic cave-like opening under a 50-foot overhang. The surrounding landscape evokes a time before European contact and includes wetlands, a waterfall, and about 150 species of native plants, including such crops as corn and tobacco.

JOSEPH HENRY STATUE. Shortly after Joseph Henry's death in 1878, Congress authorized this bronze portrait statue. Henry (1797–1878) was a professor at the College of New Jersey (later Princeton University) and a prominent scientist before becoming the first secretary of the Smithsonian Institution in 1846. A pioneer in the field of electromagnetism, Henry made an important improvement to the electromagnet, and a relief sculpture of his invention appears on the side of the monument. The statue is the work of William Wetmore Story and was dedicated in 1883. Originally, it faced the west wing of the Castle; in 1934, it was positioned to face the entrance. In May 1965, Secretary S. Dillon Ripley had the statue rotated 180 degrees to face outward, toward the Mall.

DOWNING URN. This four-foot urn was erected in 1856 to the memory of Andrew Jackson Downing (1815–1852). Downing was America's first prominent landscape architect and the author of a widely influential treatise on the subject. He was an early advocate of urban parks and a naturalistic, picturesque landscaping style. In 1850, Congress contracted Downing to landscape the Mall, but the project lost momentum in 1852 when Downing died in the sinking of the steamship *Henry Clay* (see page 12). This urn was designed by Downing's partner, architect Calvert Vaux, and executed by sculptor Robert E. Launitz. It is made of Italian marble and decorated with acanthus leaves and satyrs. It originally stood on the Mall, southeast of the present Natural History Museum, surrounded by an iron fence, until it was placed in storage in 1965. It was reinstalled adjacent to the east end of the Castle in 1972, and in 1989, it was moved to its present position in the Enid A. Haupt Garden, behind the Castle.

SPENCER BAIRD STATUE. This life-sized bronze statue of Spencer Fullerton Baird (1823–1887) stands in the Enid A. Haupt Garden, at the west entrance to the Arts and Industries building. The work of sculptor Leonard Baskin of New York, it was unveiled on May 4, 1978. Baird was the Smithsonian's second secretary and a leading authority on North American birds. He was instrumental in developing the Smithsonian as a museum (his predecessor, Joseph Henry, wanted the Smithsonian to remain as a scientific research institute), and as such, he was the first director of the U.S. National Museum, which held the Smithsonian's collections. Baird was the first U.S. Fish Commissioner (see pages 82–84), as well, and published a number of important works on North American fauna.

LEFT TO RIGHT:

Joseph Henry was the first secretary of the Smithsonian Institution and a prominent scientist.

The Downing Urn memorializes Andrew Jackson Downing, a prominent landscape architect who devised a plan for the Mall. Downing's work on the park was cut short when he perished in an 1852 steamship accident.

Spencer Baird, the Smithsonian's second secretary, helped the institution develop as a museum. His predecessor, Joseph Henry, had hoped that it would remain dedicated to scientific research.

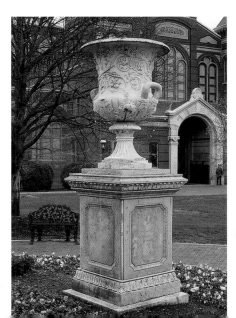

Looking east on B Street (now Constitution Avenue) from Ninth Street, c. 1900. On the left is Center Market, demolished in 1931 and today the site of the National Archives. On the right, with a tower, is the Baltimore and Potomac Railroad Station (see pages 80–81), razed in 1908.

B Street (now Constitution Avenue), looking east from Fourteenth Street, c. 1920. The dome of the National Museum, now the National Museum of Natural History, can be seen on the right, as well as four of the old Capitol gateposts. On the far left is the PEPCO power plant.

B Street (now Constitution Avenue) looking east from Fifteenth Street, c. 1920. On the left is a temporary government office building, and beyond it, with a crenelated tower and smokestacks, is the PEPCO power plant. The two buildings were demolished around 1930 for construction of the Federal Triangle project. Excavations for the new buildings uncovered remains of wharves from the time of the canal, which opened onto the Potomac at this spot prior to 1872, when it was filled in.

Constitution Avenue, known as B Street North until 1931, was not always the grand boulevard that it is today. Throughout most of the nineteenth century, it was the site of the Washington Canal, which was built for commerce, but became notorious as a reservoir of disease and filth. The city government filled in the canal in 1872, and the following year, it paved B Street for the first time.

The character of Constitution Avenue has always been determined by the Federal Triangle to the north; Pennsylvania Avenue and Fifteenth Street form the other two sides of the triangle. During the nineteenth century, this 70-acre wedge of land was prone to flooding and was relegated to marginal uses. The western end of the triangle was a notorious red-light district. Center Market, where Washingtonians shopped for food in the days before supermarkets and refrigeration, was at the eastern end. The market building covered two city blocks and housed hundreds of vendors. The portion along B Street was industrial in character, with an electric power plant, a lumber yard, and numerous market sheds.

Given its central location and rundown appearance, the Mall Triangle, as it was once known, was considered a blight on the nation's capital. The influential 1902 McMillan Plan suggested filling the triangle with buildings for the city's municipal government. The federal government, however, took over the area in the late 1920s, by buying and clearing the land. Work soon began on an array of massive federal office buildings. Many agencies had been housed in rented quarters scattered about the city, and the project lowered costs by consolidating departments into government-owned offices. Although a different architect designed each of the seven structures, all are neoclassical in style with an exterior of white stone. The last was completed in 1938.

Between 1930 and 1934, Constitution Avenue was widened and aligned, and two blocks of buildings that interrupted the avenue between Third and Sixth streets were razed. At that time, the Arlington Memorial Bridge was nearing completion, and Constitution Avenue was intended to be a great ceremonial boulevard, a

route for parades and funeral processions passing between Union Station and Arlington National Cemetery. Congress renamed B Street, N.W., Constitution Avenue in 1931, choosing the name over alternatives that included L'Enfant Avenue and Jefferson Boulevard. B Street, S.W., was renamed Independence Avenue in 1934.

Two stone gatehouses and four large stone posts now on Constitution Avenue once guarded the approaches to the Capitol. The gatehouses were built about 1829, the work of Charles Bulfinch, Architect of the Capitol. They originally stood just to the west of the Capitol, flanking a gate in a fence that surrounded the grounds. In the 1830s, the grounds were extended westward to First Street, roughly their present limit. At that time, the gatehouses were moved westward, and two additional entrances were built at Pennsylvania and Maryland avenues, each with six gateposts (see the photograph on page 55). There were 24 of these posts in all, with four posts on each of the other three sides of the grounds.

In the 1870s, the grounds of the Capitol were again enlarged and landscaped under the direction of Frederick Law Olmsted Sr. In 1873, the fence was moved to B Street North (now Constitution Avenue) where, combined with fencing of a similar pattern from Judiciary Square, it ran along the north side of the Mall from Seventh to Fifteenth Street. The fence was later removed, presumably, when Constitution Avenue was widened in the early 1930s.

Today the gatehouses stand near Constitution Avenue at Fifteenth and Seventeenth streets. Four of the posts remain: three at Fifteenth Street and one at Seventh Street. At least nine of the posts were dumped at Fort Totten; four of these were reinstalled at the National Arboretum on New York Avenue in 1991. The location of the remaining posts is unknown.

A present-day view of the Federal Triangle, looking west on Constitution Avenue from Sixth Street. Before work began on these seven massive government office buildings in 1928, the triangle was a rundown industrial area.

On the northwest corner of Fifteenth Street and Constitution Avenue are a gatehouse and gatepost that once guarded the approaches to the Capitol.

Picturesque and flamboyant, the Baltimore and Potomac Railroad Station was one of several prominent Victorian buildings that once graced the Mall. It was notorious as the site of the assassination of President James A. Garfield in 1881; as a rail depot constructed in the middle of Washington's great public park, it was controversial as well. The station was razed in 1908, and the National Gallery of Art presently occupies the site.

The Baltimore and Potomac (B&P) Railroad was a subsidiary of the great Pennsylvania Railroad, which built the B&P line into Washington to challenge its rival, the Baltimore and Ohio (B&O) Railroad. Until that time, the B&O had enjoyed a monopoly on rail service to the capital city. The B&P tracks, laid in 1871, crossed the Anacostia River and ran northwest up Virginia Avenue toward the Mall. The District government, amid allegations of corruption, gave the railroad permission to build a station on the north side of the Mall at B Street, with tracks crossing the park along Sixth Street. In 1872, Congress confirmed the District's action, and a temporary station was built on the site. Passenger service started on July 2, 1872, the same day that the new Center Market (see page 78), less than a block away, opened to the public.

Work on the B&P's elaborate new depot began in 1873. Joseph Miller Wilson of Philadelphia, a house architect for the Pennsyl-

vania Railroad, designed the building. It was High Victorian Gothic in style, with several towers asymmetrically arranged, steeply pitched roofs, and elaborate detailing. The exterior was made of patterned, pressed brick with black mortar and white sandstone banding. The roof had red, green, and blue slate arranged in geometric patterns, surmounted by delicate iron cresting. On the corner was a prominent clock tower, although no clock was ever installed. Inside, the walls had wainscoting, and there were colored tiles on the floor. Accommodations included a restaurant and three waiting rooms: one for ladies, one for gentlemen, and one general waiting room.

The station was controversial because the Pennsylvania Railroad, which had great clout in Congress, had been granted free use of a public park. The station was popular in some quarters because it was close to the city's business district, and it offered merchants relief from the B&O's monopoly on freight service. Others considered it a nuisance and an eyesore. Behind the passenger station, along Sixth Street, a 510-foot-long train shed essentially bisected the Mall. Steam trains chugged slowly through the park, belching soot and disrupting the otherwise bucolic atmosphere. Often-

RIGHT. The Baltimore and Potomac Railroad Station, looking south on Sixth Street, November 1906. The ornate structure stood on the site of the present-day National Gallery of Art before being razed in 1908.

The assassination of President James A. Garfield in the Baltimore and Potomac Railroad Station, on July 2, 1881, was certainly the most momentous event ever to occur on the National Mall. In this print, the assassin Charles Guiteau fires a revolver at Garfield, striking him in the back. Secretary of State James G. Blaine appears on the right.

times, long strings of cars blocked carriage traffic at grade crossings.

On July 2, 1881, President James A. Garfield, who had been in office only four months, was assassinated in the Baltimore and Potomac Railroad Station. The president was passing through the ladies' waiting room with Secretary of State James G. Blaine when assassin Charles Guiteau shot him in the back with a revolver. Garfield fell to the floor, wounded but still conscious. He was taken first to a room upstairs and then to the White House.

Garfield lingered for 80 days before he died, the victim of slow blood poisoning. His doctors probed the wound with unwashed hands, although antiseptic technique was already in practice and might have saved his life. Garfield's long struggle, and his death on September 19, was attended with more public anguish than the assassination of Abraham Lincoln. Two weeks before his death, Garfield was moved to his summer home in Elberon, New Jersey. As his train made its way north, citizens lined the route, hats in hand, many in tears.

Guiteau, the assassin, had campaigned for Garfield and believed that he deserved a public appointment in return, perhaps as consul general to Paris. He came to Washington and made numerous unsuccessful attempts to speak to Garfield about the matter. Mentally deranged, he obsessed over Garfield's widely publicized confrontation with fellow Republican Roscoe Conkling, a powerful senator from New York. Guiteau feared that Garfield was destroying the Republican party and became convinced that it was God's will that he remove him from office.

After the assassination, Guiteau was quickly apprehended and, after a trial, hanged in the old D.C. jail. A star was installed in the floor of the depot to mark the spot where Garfield was mortally wounded, and a plaque was mounted on the wall. Today, the site of the assassination would be on Constitution Avenue in front of the National Gallery of Art, but there is no indication of the events that took place there in 1881.

The station's demise began as the McMillan Commission developed its plan for the improvement of Washington's parks. The commission naturally proposed removing the depot from the Mall,

but it recognized that the Pennsylvania Railroad's consent would be needed, given its great influence with Congress. Fortuitously, the Pennsylvania Railroad and the B&O merged as the McMillan Plan was still under development, and there was no longer a need for two stations. Andrew Cassatt, president of the Pennsylvania Railroad, was willing to abandon the Mall site if Congress helped pay for a new station north of the Capitol. Congress agreed, and the new depot, named Union Station because it unified both lines, opened in 1907. The old B&P station was demolished the following year.

Looking north across the Mall on Sixth Street from Maryland Avenue, S.W., c. 1900. The footbridge crossing over Sixth Street stood on what is now the site of the National Air and Space Museum. Beyond is the clock tower of the Baltimore and Potomac Railroad Station.

In 1918, the Ordnance building, a temporary office building for war workers, was constructed on the site of the Baltimore and Potomac Railroad Station.

Although the Fish Commission was a fixture on the Mall for more than a half century, its presence there is all but forgotten today. The commission had its headquarters in the old Washington Armory, located on the present-day site of the National Air and Space Museum, and it maintained fish ponds on the grounds of the Washington Monument.

Congress created the U.S. Commission of Fish and Fisheries in 1871 to investigate a decline in American fish stocks. The new commission was placed under the auspices of the Smithsonian Institution, and Spencer F. Baird, then assistant secretary of the Smithsonian, became the first commissioner.

The Fish Commission soon established administrative and research facilities at Woods Hole, Massachusetts. Between 1881 and 1882, the headquarters moved to Washington, occupying the old Washington Armory on the northwest corner of B Street South (now Independence Avenue) and Sixth Street.

The old armory became known as the Fisheries building. Experiments in fish culture were conducted there, and fish were hatched by the millions to replenish native stocks and introduce new species to American waters. A short siding connected the building to the nearby Baltimore and Potomac Railroad, and special railcars carried eggs and young fish to all parts of the country. Among many other projects, the Fish Commission successfully introduced shad into the rivers of the western United States.

The Fish Commission had a small aquarium in its building on the Mall, which opened to the public in 1888. Fish and other marine animals were on display in large tanks, and there were exhibits on the fishing industry, fish hatching, and so on. That same year, the Fish Commission left the Smithsonian and became an independent agency. In 1903, it joined the new Department of Commerce and was renamed the Bureau of Fisheries. Over time, the old armory became woefully inadequate, and Bureau of Fisheries officials lobbied for a new building, a "national aquarium" that would be worthy of the name.

In 1932, the bureau left the Mall, moving into the new Department of Commerce building in the Federal Triangle. An aquarium was built in the basement of the enormous building, and the fish were

The old Washington Armory was headquarters for the Fish Commission for 50 years. In the foreground of this 1891 photograph is a railcar specially outfitted for the transport of fish eggs and fry. Today, the National Air and Space Museum occupies the site.

Removing young carp from sluiceways at Fish Lakes Station, 1891. The Fish Commission planted carp in waters all over the United States, hoping to popularize it as a food fish. Fish Lakes Station was on the grounds of the Washington Monument. In this photograph, the Bureau of Engraving and Printing is visible on the horizon.

ABOVE. Removing roe from salmon at Fish Lakes Station. The old lockhouse at Seventeenth Street and Constitution Avenue is visible in the background. The blue photographic prints are known as cyanotypes.

LEFT. The fish ponds, seen here from the corner of Constitution Avenue and Seventeenth Street, c. 1900, were a place of great scenic beauty.

moved there from the old building. The National Aquarium is still in operation to this day, at the same location (on Fourteenth Street between Constitution and Pennsylvania avenues), although it has been privately operated since 1982 due to federal budget cuts. (In 2003, it became affiliated with the much larger *National Aquarium in Baltimore*, which was built by the City of Baltimore and opened in 1982.) The Fish Commission lives on in its descendants, the U.S. Fish and Wildlife Service, and the National Marine Fisheries Service.

During the nineteenth century, the Fish Commission established stations around the country where fish were raised for distribution to lakes and rivers. Such a station was established between 1877 and 1878 on the northwest corner of the grounds of the Washington Monument, where several existing ponds were adapted to the purposes of the commission. Carp, bass, and other fish, plus dozens of species of turtles, were raised there. The ponds were open to the public, and visitors could see a wide variety of aquatic plants, in addition to marine life.

Over the years, as the landscaping of the Mall was improved, the grounds of the fish ponds were improved as well, and they became a place of great scenic beauty. There was a house for the superintendent of the station, a building for preparing fish for shipment, a watchman's lodge, and other buildings. Fish Lakes Station, as it was known, was closed in 1906, when the Bureau of Fisheries found it too expensive to maintain. Between 1907 and 1910, one of the fish ponds was used by the city government as a public swimming basin. In 1910, the city built some cement swimming pools on the site, and they remained in operation until 1935.

The Washington Armory, or the Fisheries building as it was known for many years, was completed in 1857 for the District of Columbia militia. During the Civil War, it was the main building of Armory Square Hospital, a large installation with dozens of wooden buildings that extended halfway across the Mall between Fifth and Seventh streets. The hospital was dismantled after the war, and the armory remained empty for about a decade. In 1877 it was transferred to the Smithsonian, which used the building to store some exhibits from the 1876 Centennial Exhibition until the Arts and Industries building could be completed. After the armory was vacated by the Bureau of Fisheries in 1932, it served a number of undistinguished functions before being demolished in 1964.

This 1911 photograph, from a family album, gives a rare view of the public swimming pools constructed on the site of Fish Lakes Station after it closed. The building had been the home of the station superintendent and his family.

For almost a century, the Army Medical Museum welcomed visitors to the Mall with a macabre collection of medical specimens. Exhibits open to the public included a collection of abnormal babies preserved in glass jars, organs with bullet wounds or ravaged by disease, and the world's largest collection of microscopes. Also on display were the bullet that killed Abraham Lincoln and the vertebra of President James Garfield pierced by the assassin's bullet. Garfield had been shot in the Baltimore and Potomac Railroad Station, directly across the Mall.

In 1862, the Army Medical Museum was established as a place where pathologic material from the Civil War could be gathered and used for research. It occupied several sites, the last being Ford's Theater on Tenth Street, N.W., before moving to the Mall in 1887. The new building, designed by Adolph Cluss, was built of brick in the Romanesque Revival style.

The Army Medical Museum became the military's center for pathologic research. Walter Reed was curator from 1893 until his death in 1902, and during this time he proved that yellow fever was transmitted by mosquitoes. Important work on typhoid fever was also performed at the museum. It served as a national repository for pathologic specimens and had a medical school and a large library, as well.

After World War II, the museum was reorganized as the Armed Forces Institute of Pathology, with the public museum as only one component. In the 1950s, the exhibits were housed in a wartime temporary building across Independence Avenue, while the main building served other purposes.

In 1969, the museum building was demolished in spite of its designation as a National Historic Landmark. Financier and art collector Joseph Hirshhorn had offered the Smithsonian a superb collection of modern art, with the stipulation that it be located on the Mall, and the Army Medical Museum occupied a choice site. The museum was moved to the grounds of the Walter Reed Army Medical Center on Georgia Avenue, N.W., where it remains today. It has been renamed several times, most recently as the National Museum of Health and Medicine, in 1989.

TOP. The Army Medical Museum, c. 1920, looking north across Independence Avenue from Seventh Street, S.W. The building was demolished in 1969 for the construction of the Hirshhorn Museum.

BOTTOM. The second floor exhibit hall, c. 1910. During World War II, the museum boasted the world's largest medical library.

Looking north from the old Agriculture building toward the commercial heart of Washington, c. 1875. In the foreground is a terrace with a formal garden, bordered on the north by a balustrade and two elaborate iron pavilions. Beyond the terrace, the grounds were laid out as an arboretum, with winding paths and a wide variety of trees grouped according to their scientific classification.

RIGHT. When the Department of Agriculture was formed in 1862, it took control of a propagating garden that the Patent Office had established on the Mall in 1856. The garden was north of the canal between Four and One-Half and Sixth streets, and this building was the office of the superintendent. In 1867, the National Grange was formed here as a fraternal organization for farmers, and today a plaque marks the spot. In 1873, the garden was cleared and its functions moved to Agriculture's main reservation on the Mall.

The imposing marble façade of the Agriculture building stretches 750 feet along the south side of the Mall, opposite the National Museum of American History. Headquarters for a cabinet-level department with 100,000 employees, it is the only major structure on the Mall that is not open to the public.

The Department of Agriculture has "owned" this site since 1863, when Congress awarded it the entire square between Twelfth and Fourteenth streets. In 1868, a new headquarters building was completed, designed in the Second Empire style by architects Adolph Cluss and Joseph von Kammerhueber. The exterior was made of pressed brick with ornate brownstone trim, while the interior was elaborately finished with fine wood paneling and frescoes. An agricultural museum occupied the second floor. Visitors could see fruits and vegetables modeled in plaster, samples of various woods and natural fibers, and many other interesting and educational exhibits.

The present main Agriculture building was constructed between 1904 and 1930. Its location was the subject of a bitter dispute between Secretary of Agriculture James Wilson and proponents of the 1902 McMillan Plan for the city's parks. The secretary hoped to place his building much closer to the centerline of the Mall than would have been permitted. However, the plan's supporters staunchly believed that no exceptions should be made. Charles McKim, an architect who had served on the McMillan Commission, took the dispute to President Theodore Roosevelt, whom he knew well through his work on the renovations to the White House. Roosevelt overruled Secretary Wilson, setting an important precedent in favor of the McMillan Plan.

Top. The old brick Agriculture building, c. 1875. Completed in 1868, the building served as headquarters for the Department of Agriculture and housed an agricultural museum. It was razed in 1930.

Bottom left. Beside the old Agriculture building was a 320-foot-long conservatory, built around 1870. The center pavilion held palms and other large tropical plants, while the wings had semitropical fruits, "useful" plants, and foreign grapes. It was razed around 1904.

Bottom center. The Redwood Tree House was a hollow section of an immense giant sequoia, 26 feet in diameter. It was cut in California in 1892 for display at the World's Columbian Exposition in Chicago. In 1894, the trunk was reinstalled on the Agriculture grounds. Visitors could mount a circular staircase inside the tree and view the grounds from the four windows. It was removed in 1932.

Bottom right. A horse-drawn streetcar heads north across the Mall on Twelfth Street, c. 1890. In the background are the densely planted grounds of the Department of Agriculture.

The architectural firm of Rankin, Kellogg and Crane designed the building in the Beaux-Arts style. The initial appropriation from Congress was too small to pay for the entire building, so the wings were built first, between 1904 and 1908. The central portion was not begun until 1927, two decades later! During the intervening years, the marble wings of the unfinished building and the old brick Agriculture headquarters stood together incongruously on the Mall. To cut costs, the center section of the new building was finished in a simpler style than originally planned, and a large dome was omitted. It was completed in 1930, and the old headquarters was demolished the same year.

Today it is little appreciated that the Agriculture Department was once an important tourist attraction. Besides the museum, there was a large iron-and-glass conservatory just to the west of the old main building that displayed a large variety of plants. William Saunders, superintendent of the Agriculture gardens and a nationally prominent landscape architect and horticulturist, designed the grounds. Saunders planted the northern portion (now the site of the American History Museum) as an arboretum, grouping trees and shrubs informally, according to their botanical classifications. Directly in

front of the building was a formal French-inspired garden decorated with sculpture, and behind it was an experimental garden. Curved paths wound through the grounds, and it became a popular spot for Washingtonians to go for a stroll or a carriage drive.

A row of greenhouses was erected on the north end of the grounds in 1904. These were joined by other buildings until the entire north side bordering B Street (now Constitution Avenue) was lined with a motley assortment of structures. Some of the buildings were open to the public, and there were demonstrations of various agricultural skills. On the south side of the grounds there were a number of other ancillary structures. These were demolished between 1904 and 1930, as the present main Agriculture building was built.

In the 1930s, Agriculture transferred a large swath of its reservation to the National Park Service. Subsequently, the elaborate Victorian-era garden was plowed under, and a broad lawn bordered by rows of elms was planted. In 1940, the buildings on the north side of the grounds were demolished and soon replaced with wartime temporary buildings; these, in turn, were razed in 1958 for the new American History Museum.

Top. The present main Agriculture building, seen here about 1937, holds the offices of the secretary of agriculture. The center portion is Georgia marble, the wings are Vermont marble, and the base is Massachusetts granite.

Bottom. The main building of the Department of Agriculture (left) is on the Mall. It is connected to the South Building (right) by two bridges that span Independence Avenue. The wings of the main building were built between 1904 and 1908, while the center portion was not completed until 1930. The South Building was finished in 1937.

LEFT. Robert Mills's design for the Washington Monument was accepted in 1845. It called for a 600-foot obelisk surrounded by a pantheon, 250 feet in diameter. Work began on the obelisk in 1848, but due to a lack of funds, the pantheon was never built.

RIGHT. Construction of the obelisk stopped at the 156-foot level for more than 20 years. This photograph was taken in 1879 as work resumed. The original foundations, pictured here, had to be reinforced with concrete.

George Washington (1732–1799) was the commander of the American armies in the Revolutionary War, presided over the Constitutional Convention in 1787, and was the first president of the United States. His character was regarded as beyond reproach. During his life he was venerated; after his death he was virtually deified.

In 1783, the Continental Congress resolved that an equestrian statue of Washington be erected in the nation's permanent capital. When Peter Charles L'Enfant drew up a plan for the new city in 1791, he provided a site for the statue where the axes of the "Congress House" and the "President's House" intersected. The statue was never realized, but the site was later used for the Washington Monument.

In the decades to follow, there were numerous attempts to establish a monument to Washington in the new capital. In 1833 a group of citizens formed the Washington National Monument Society to provide a proper monument to the first president. The society held a design competition in 1836, but none of the entries was acceptable. In 1845, the society adopted a design by architect Robert Mills. The scheme called for a 600-foot obelisk surrounded by a pantheon, 100 feet high and 250 feet in diameter. The monument would be decorated with statues, historical paintings, and bas-relief sculpture. Immense, ornate, and destined to be the tallest building in the world, the society saw the monument as commensurate with the stature of Washington and the American nation. By 1848, enough money had been collected to begin work, and Congress authorized the society to use the site specified by L'Enfant. To save money, the obelisk would be built first, and the pantheon, later.

Presumably because of poor soil conditions, the monument was built somewhat to the southeast of L'Enfant's site, a decision that would have repercussions later, when the Mall was extended westward. Mills was hired to supervise construction, and excavations were completed early in 1848. On July 4, 1848, the cornerstone was laid in a grand ceremony. Present were President James K. Polk, many members of Congress and other dignitaries, U.S. Marines, militia and fire companies, and perhaps 20,000 spectators, including a contingent of aged Revolutionary War veterans. Perched on a decorated arch was an eagle that had witnessed Lafayette's triumphant return to America 24 years earlier.

The foundations and the interior of the shaft were constructed of gneiss; the exterior, of white marble from a quarry near the town of Texas, Maryland. The society received decorative memorial stones from all over the world, which were installed in the interior, facing the stairwell. Stones were contributed by states, territories, foreign countries, fraternal organizations, and many other sources. There are about 200 stones in all, some installed after the completion of the monument.

In 1854, the society ran out of money, and progress on the shaft stopped at 152 feet. That same year, members of the nativist and anti-Catholic Know-Nothing party stole a stone given by the Vatican and reportedly dumped it into the Potomac River. In February

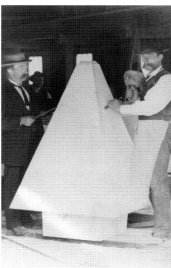

ABOVE. A worker puts finishing touches on the 3,300-pound marble capstone. Its installation on December 6, 1884, marked the completion of the monument. At the tip of the capstone was a 100-ounce pyramid of aluminum, at that time the largest aluminum casting ever made.

LEFT. The monument was dedicated on February 21, 1885, a frigid day in Washington. It was the tallest building in the world, a distinction it would hold for five years.

1855 the party seized control of the Washington National Monument Society. During the three years that they controlled the society, the Know-Nothings added only four feet to the obelisk, and the work was of such low quality that the stones were later removed. Progress on the monument stalled at the 156-foot level, and it would remain an unsightly stump for more than 20 years.

In July 1876, in celebration of the nation's centennial, Congress appropriated funds for the completion of the monument. Control of the stump passed from the society to the federal government, and

the U.S. Army Corps of Engineers was charged with its completion. Work resumed in 1878, with Lieutenant Colonel Thomas Lincoln Casey directing the project.

Casey found the 1848 foundations woefully inadequate and reinforced them with concrete, a delicate operation. The new foundations rest on a firm bed of sand, gravel, and clay, but they do not extend to bedrock.

When work resumed, the finished height of the shaft was still in question. George Perkins Marsh, the U.S. minister to Italy, suggested that the proper height should be 10 times the width of the base, a proportion derived from close examination of Egyptian obelisks in Rome. Casey adopted Marsh's suggestions, and the finished height of the monument is 555 feet 5⅛ inches.

Work resumed on the shaft in August 1880. Initially, Casey used white marble from Sheffield, Massachusetts, for the exterior, but after only a few courses, he switched to marble from Cockeysville, Maryland. The Cockeysville marble is a slightly different color, easily perceptible today. For the interior of the shaft, he used granite from Maine. Work proceeded rapidly, and by August 1884, the shaft had reached the 500-foot level.

On December 6, 1884, Casey set the 3,300-pound capstone,

LEFT. The Washington Monument, c. 1885. At the time, the Potomac River was only 1,000 feet from the base of the monument. The Army Corps of Engineers was busy dredging the channel and filling the shoreline, and a dredge can be seen to the left of the shaft. When the monument was completed, marble shutters covered the windows to preserve the geometric purity of the obelisk. They were removed a short time later.

RIGHT. The Washington Monument, c. 1900. The small lodge in the foreground was completed in 1889.

OPPOSITE. The Washington Monument is a landmark visible throughout much of the city.

completing the monument. A small ceremony marked the occasion. At the tip of the capstone was a 100-ounce pyramid of pure aluminum. In 1884, refining and casting pure aluminum was very difficult, and this was the largest such casting of its time. The pyramid was intended as a lightning conductor, but it was soon supplemented with an array of copper rods.

The Washington Monument was dedicated on February 21, 1885. It was the tallest building in the world, surpassing Cologne Cathedral in Germany. Within five years, the monument was itself surpassed by the Eiffel Tower, but it remains the tallest masonry structure in the world.

The monument was officially opened to the public in 1888. Visitors could ascend the shaft by traveling in a steam-driven elevator or by climbing the 896 steps. In 1901, the elevator was replaced with one powered by electricity. At the 500-foot level there is an observation platform with eight openings that offer an excellent view of the city. In the 1920s, after several suicides, the openings were fitted with bars, and bulletproof glass was installed in 1974. The stairs were closed to the public in the 1970s.

Between 1998 and 2001, the monument underwent a thorough restoration. Elaborate scaffolding, designed by architect Michael Graves, encased the obelisk for more than a year while the exterior was cleaned and the stonework was repaired. Inside, the memorial stones were restored, the observation deck was refurbished, and a new elevator was installed.

In 1998, in the wake of terrorist attacks on two American embassies in Africa, the National Park Service installed a ring of Jersey barriers around the monument, which remained for five years. In 2003, the Park Service placed surveillance cameras in four of the windows, but removed them within three years. In 2005, work was completed on a permanent vehicle barrier, a ring of low granite walls about 400 feet from the shaft. At the same time, the monument grounds were improved with new grading, paths, lighting, benches, and trees. An underground visitor center, which would have required tourists to enter the monument through a long tunnel, was under consideration, but was ultimately canceled.

The Capitol Stone, seen here during an 1881 flood, stood southwest of the Washington Monument. It was installed in 1804 to assist with the placement of the Jefferson Stone and was so-named because it was due west of the southern end of the original Capitol building. It disappeared around 1890.

This monument marks the site of the Jefferson Stone, which stood here between 1804 and 1872. Recent research by Silvio Bedini revealed that the missing part of the inscription was "being the centre point of the," which was no doubt chiseled away because it was incorrect. The true center point of the district lies near Seventeenth and C streets, N.W.

Anondescript stone marker, erected in 1889, stands a short distance to the northwest of the Washington Monument. It marks the original location of the Jefferson Stone, a masonry pier constructed many years earlier as part of Thomas Jefferson's attempt to locate a national prime meridian in Washington. One might assume that the original Jefferson pier was a dock or wharf, given that this site lay on the river's edge before landfill operations greatly extended the park. Rather, the word *pier* used here denotes a heavy square column.

The prime meridian is the line of 0 degrees of longitude from which all others are calculated. Today, it passes through the Royal Observatory in Greenwich, England, a standard that has been accepted worldwide for more than a century. At the time of Jefferson's administration, however, many countries hoped to establish their own prime meridians. America was no exception, and Jefferson wanted to reinforce the country's independence from England by creating a new prime meridian that would pass through the White House.

In October 1804, Nicholas King, the city's surveyor, installed the Jefferson Stone at the exact spot where a north–south line drawn through the center of the White House would intersect an east–west line drawn through the Capitol. The stone, constructed of several slabs of Aquia sandstone filled with rubble, was intended to mark the new prime meridian. It was located on what was then the riverbank where Tiber Creek emptied into the Potomac and can clearly be seen in the 1851 drawing by Seth Eastman that is reproduced on page 11.

Over time, the original purpose of the Jefferson Stone was forgotten. In 1872, Orville Babcock of the U.S. Army Corps of Engineers removed the stone as part of improvements to the grounds of the Washington Monument and buried the foundations under landfill. Unfortunately, the stone had been used as a benchmark in a number of early land surveys, and its location would later prove to be important in the Potomac Flats case, a court case that established the ownership of lands along the riverfront. The U.S. attorney general ordered that the Jefferson Stone be located and restored, and the present stone marker, installed in 1889, is the result.

The National Park Service and its predecessors used a propagating garden, once located just south of the Washington Monument, to cultivate trees, shrubs, and other plants for the city's parks. Despite the fact that the garden endured for more than a century, it is all but forgotten today.

Prior to 1867, the Mall was the responsibility of the commissioner of public buildings, whose duties included selling lots in the city and maintaining the White House, the Capitol, and other public buildings and parks. In 1851, the commissioner established a propagating garden southeast of the Capitol roughly on the site of the present-day Capitol Heating Plant. In 1857, he moved the garden to the Mall, where it occupied a triangular lot between Third and Four and One-Half streets, north of the canal. (It was just to the east of the Department of Agriculture's propagating garden; see page 86.) A tourist's guidebook described its prodigious output:

In 1872 ... upwards of 20,000 papers of flower seeds were collected and cured. These, with surplus plants, sometimes numbering upwards of 10,000 consisting of roses, chrysanthemums, verbenas, geraniums, begonias, and other hot-house annuals and shrubs propagated at these gardens, were distributed to members of Congress, and others notified by circular letter that such stock was ready. A Nursery is connected with the garden, in which trees and shrubs are grown for the supply of the public parks.

In 1867, the commissioner's duties were transferred to the U.S. Army Corps of Engineers. The engineers soon undertook an ambitious program for the improvement of the Mall and, in 1873, moved the propagating garden to the grounds of the Washington Monument. The eight-acre site was located on what was then the banks of the Potomac, now the Tidal Basin.

The National Park Service assumed responsibility for the propagating garden when it took over the Mall in 1933. The garden grew considerably over the years, and by 1942, there were 33 greenhouses. The glass houses were dismantled that same year as a wartime budgetary measure, and the materials were given to the war effort. The propagating garden served as a maintenance yard for the Park Service until the remaining buildings were razed in 1962, and the area was relandscaped as a park.

An aerial view of the propagating garden (center foreground), looking south from the Washington Monument, 1898. On the left is the future site of the Bureau of Engraving and Printing. In the background is the Washington Channel (left), the Tidal Basin (right), and East Potomac Park.

Commemorating the American victory in the central event of the twentieth century, the National World War II Memorial honors the sacrifices of the 16 million Americans who served in the war, the 400,000 who died, and millions of others who aided the war effort on the home front. The memorial occupies an important, and controversial, site directly between the Washington Monument and the Lincoln Memorial.

The main entrance is on the east, facing the Washington Monument. Visitors descend a wide staircase to the Rainbow Pool, where jets of water spray into the air. The pool is set in the center of a broad granite plaza, six feet below grade. From this vantage point, the Mall is no longer visible, and the visitor is surrounded by two semicircles of monumental pillars. On the opposite side of the plaza is a wall of gold stars flanked by two waterfalls. There are 4,048 stars, one for every hundred Americans who died in the war.

Congress passed legislation authorizing the memorial in May 1993. By that time, veterans of the Korean and Vietnam wars had been recognized by memorials on the Mall, and it seemed appropriate that there should be one for veterans of World War II. Congress gave the job of establishing the memorial to the American Battle Monuments Commission (ABMC), a federal agency that maintains military cemeteries and monuments around the world.

The ABMC initially chose a site in Constitution Gardens, just to the north of the Rainbow Pool, but it was rejected by the Commission of Fine Arts (CFA) at a July 1995 hearing. J. Carter Brown, the commission's chairman, believed that the site, located in a wooded park on the sidelines of the Mall, did not do justice to an event of the magnitude of World War II. Instead, he suggested the Rainbow Pool, a far more visible location astride the main axis of the Mall. The ABMC embraced the new site, and it was approved that same year.

The ABMC then set about securing a design for the memorial. It held a competition, selecting a design by Austrian-born architect Friedrich St.Florian of Providence, Rhode Island, from among more than 400 entries. When St.Florian's design was presented to the CFA in July 1997, several important components were disapproved. His original design had 50 columns backed by two earthen

The Rainbow Pool, in the foreground, is the site of the new World War II Memorial. This photograph was taken from the Washington Monument, c. 1925, shortly after the completion of the Lincoln Memorial.

Friedrich St.Florian's original competition-winning design for the World War II Memorial included 50 columns and two massive berms, features that were later eliminated as the design was refined. The berms were intended to hide four rooms that might have held a small museum.

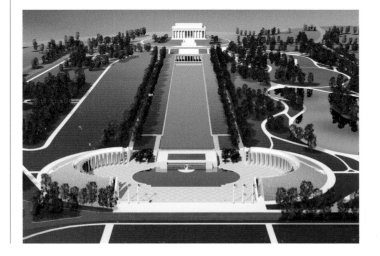

berms, each 50 feet tall, which concealed four rooms (see the rendering on the opposite page). In May 1998, St.Florian returned to the CFA with a revised design for the memorial. The berms and the rooms were gone, and the 50 columns had been replaced with a low wall topped with a metal screen. The perimeter wall was subsequently replaced with granite pillars, each with two bronze wreaths. The design received final approval in 2000.

In October 2000, a coalition of groups opposed to the memorial and its location on the Mall's main axis filed a lawsuit blocking construction. A groundbreaking ceremony took place on November 11, but in reality, the assembled dignitaries sank their shovels into a ceremonial trough of dirt, and work would not begin for almost a year. In May 2001, exasperated by the delays, Congress passed a bill directing that the construction of the memorial begin immediately, immune to any legal challenges. Work began in August 2001, although many details of the design remained to be settled.

The memorial is built of granite, with a concrete foundation. The stone for the vertical elements is from Georgia, while the paving stones are from South Carolina, and the green accent stone is from Brazil. The Rainbow Pool was demolished and reconstructed 15 percent smaller in size.

Raymond Kaskey, of Washington, D.C., was responsible for the sculptural elements. Lining the main entrance to the memorial are 24 bas-relief panels. Each of these bronze sculptures, 5½ feet wide and 2 feet tall, bears a different scene from the war, expressively rendered and accurate in its historical detail. Each of the two pavilions has a sculptural group comprising four eagles holding a laurel wreath, which symbolizes victory. On each of the 56 pillars there are two bronze wreaths, one of oak leaves, symbolizing America's industrial might, and one of wheat, symbolizing agriculture.

Leo A Daly, an architectural and engineering firm, translated St.Florian's design into detailed plans for the memorial. The construction work was performed by a joint venture between Tompkins Builders and Grunley-Walsh Construction, both based in the Washington area. The landscaping of the 7.4-acre site was designed by Oehme, van Sweden & Associates, of Washington, D.C., a landscape architectural firm.

The dedication ceremony for the memorial was held on May 29, 2004, and more than 150,000 people attended. At the ceremony, President George W. Bush accepted the memorial on behalf of the American people from General Paul X. Kelley, a retired Marine Corps officer and chairman of the ABMC.

The World War II Memorial seen from the east shortly before its dedication. The memorial cost approximately $175 million to build. The funds were raised almost entirely through private donations. At each end of the memorial is a granite pavilion, one inscribed "Atlantic," the other "Pacific," for the two theaters of the war. Flanking each pavilion is a semicircle of pillars. There are 56 in all, one for each state and territory at the time of the war, plus the District of Columbia.

LEFT. The names on the wall are arranged chronologically by date of death, starting at the vertex with the first American casualty in 1959.

RIGHT. The Vietnam Women's Memorial, by Glenna Goodacre, acknowledges the contributions of women who served in the war.

BOTTOM. *The Three Servicemen*, by Frederick Hart, addressed critics' concerns that the memorial should be demonstrably patriotic.

The Vietnam War ended in 1975. Compared with other monuments on the Mall, the memorial to those who served in Vietnam was realized with extraordinary speed, although its design was almost as controversial as the war itself.

The Vietnam Veterans Memorial Fund (VVMF), a private organization, was formed in 1979 to fund the memorial and see it to completion. In 1981, after a competition that drew a record 1,421 entries, the jury selected a design by Maya Lin (see page 43), then a 21-year-old architecture student at Yale University. Lin's design featured a V-shaped black granite wall set into the earth. One arm of the wall would be aligned with the Washington Monument, and the other, with the Lincoln Memorial. The names of those who died or remained missing would be inscribed on the wall.

The VVMF required that the memorial be politically neutral toward the war. Some critics felt that Lin's proposal was antiwar, an expression of shame and sorrow that dishonored those who had died, not one of pride and patriotism. These objections were overcome by adding a flagpole and a sculpture to the memorial. The placement of these new elements was itself controversial, and ultimately, they were located at the west entrance, where they have minimal impact on the integrity of Lin's design.

Ground was broken in March 1982, and the memorial was dedicated on November 13 that year. Each arm of the wall is 247 feet long and comprises 74 black granite slabs. Names are occasionally added to the wall, and as of Memorial Day 2006, there were 58,253 names.

Lin intended that the memorial be experienced by descending into it, not as a static object to be viewed from afar. Indeed, a chain railing forces visitors into intimate contact with the wall, where their reflections in the black granite merge with the names of the dead. A visit to the wall is a moving experience. Perhaps the memorial's success lies in the fact that it makes no judgment about the war, leaving it open to individual interpretation.

The commission for the sculpture went to Frederick Hart. Dedicated in 1984, Hart's work is a realistic depiction of three soldiers, two white and one black. Criticism that Hart's statue did not include a figural portrayal of a woman, many of whom served in Vietnam, led to the establishment of the Vietnam Women's Memorial, a narrative sculptural group by Glenna Goodacre. Located in the woods to the southeast of the wall, it was dedicated in 1993.

Dedicated in 1995, the Korean War Veterans Memorial lies a short distance to the southeast of the Lincoln Memorial. It honors those who served in the Korean War, a conflict that began in June 1950 when North Korean forces, later backed by Chinese troops, invaded South Korea. Over three years, the United States, fighting under the United Nations flag with 21 other nations, fought the war to a stalemate.

If the experience of visiting the Vietnam Veterans Memorial is a somber communion with the dead, the Korean War Veterans Memorial is meant to evoke patriotism and the travails of the 1.5 million Americans who served in Korea. At the center of the memorial is the triangular Field of Service, where 19 statues of American soldiers, marines, and airmen walk up a gentle slope toward an American flag. The statues are the work of sculptor Frank Gaylord, of Barre, Vermont, himself a veteran of World War II.

Seven and a half feet tall and made of stainless steel, the men are alert yet weary, draped in ponchos, and staggering under heavy loads against the weather. There is danger in the air, and they com-municate among themselves through glances and words on open lips. They peer into the distance, drawing the visitor into the drama.

Along one side of the field is a black granite wall, the work of graphic designer Louis Nelson of New York. Sandblasted into the wall are the faces of men and women—the doctors, nurses, truck drivers, clerks, and many others—who supported the combat troops. About 1,200 in number, their arrangement is reminiscent of an Asian scroll painting.

At the head of the wall is the legend "Freedom Is Not Free" inlaid in silver. On the opposite side of the field is a curb with the names of the 22 allied nations. The wall and the curb join, inter-secting a circular Pool of Remembrance, which is ringed with trees. Nearby are inscribed the numbers of American and United Nations dead, wounded, captured, and missing.

Congress authorized the memorial in 1986. Three years later, a jury selected a design by a team of four architects, all faculty mem-bers at Pennsylvania State University. Cooper-Lecky Architects of Washington, D.C., was hired to supervise the project. As the proj-ect progressed, the design was radically altered, and the four com-petition winners dropped out of the process after losing a lawsuit to block the changes. Ulti-mately, the memorial was a collaboration among many parties, but principally Cooper-Lecky, Gaylord, and the Commission of Fine Arts, which had authority over the design and loca-tion of the memorial.

The original design had 38 statues, for the armistice line at the 38th parallel, and the war, which ended in its 38th month. The number of statues was later reduced by half at the sugges-tion of the Commission of Fine Arts. President George H. W. Bush broke ground for the me-morial in 1992. It was dedicated on July 27, 1995, the 42nd anniversary of the armistice that ended the war, by President Bill Clinton and President Kim Young Sam of South Korea.

Frank Gaylord's sculptures capture the weariness and tension of troops in battle.

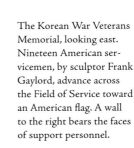

The Korean War Veterans Memorial, looking east. Nineteen American ser-vicemen, by sculptor Frank Gaylord, advance across the Field of Service toward an American flag. A wall to the right bears the faces of support personnel.

As late as 1960, there were still more than a dozen wartime "temporary" buildings on the Mall. Built as offices for government workers during World War I and II, the last was not demolished until 1970!

More than a dozen "tempos" went up on the Mall in World War I. The largest was the Navy building, built near the site of the reflecting pool in 1918, containing more than 1 million square feet of office space. Most of the World War I tempos were demolished in the decades after the war.

During World War II, more than 50 tempos were built in the District and Arlington, concentrated along the Mall and in West Potomac Park. While the World War I tempos were generally built of reinforced concrete, those constructed during World II were made of wood. The Department of the Interior opposed such large-scale construction in Washington's parks—millions of dollars were spent in the 1930s landscaping the Mall—to little effect.

The tempos were supposed to have been demolished immediately after World War II, but the Cold War kept demand for office space high, and Congress was slow to provide funds for permanent buildings. Most of the tempos on the Mall were finally razed in the 1960s.

OPPOSITE. During World War II, temporary buildings filled Potomac Park. On the right are barracks for WAVES, women naval personnel.

CLOCKWISE (from top left):

Looking east on Constitution Avenue toward Seventeenth Street, c. 1925. The Munitions building (foreground) and the Navy building (background) were the last "temporary" buildings on the Mall. Constructed during World War I, they were not demolished until 1970.

Bridges connected the Navy building on Constitution Avenue with an annex across the reflecting pool. The bridges were constructed during World War II and demolished shortly thereafter.

Wartime temporary buildings occupied the site of the present-day National Air and Space Museum in 1962. On the left is the Army Medical Museum and Seventh Street; on the right is Independence Avenue.

Temporary Building E, built during World War I, stood on the Mall until July 1970. In the foreground is Sixth Street; to the left is Adams Drive, converted to a gravel path in 1975.

Constitution Gardens, a 45-acre park located between the reflecting pool and Constitution Avenue, was dedicated in May 1976 to mark the national bicentennial. The highlight is a six-acre artificial lake, three feet deep. An island, accessible by a bridge, is the site of a small memorial to the 56 signers of the Declaration of Independence. The memorial has an arc of granite blocks, each inscribed with a replica of the signature of one of the signers, surrounding a small granite plaza. It was dedicated on July 2, 1984.

The architectural firm of Skidmore, Owings and Merrill designed the park as a picturesque garden, with winding paths and informally scattered trees and bushes. It was intended as a spot for weary tourists to rest on the long trek between the Washington Monument and the Lincoln Memorial.

The park replaced the Navy and Munitions buildings (see page 101), which were demolished in 1970. Work began on the park in 1974 and was completed within two years. A café planned for the eastern end of the lake was eliminated to lower costs, but terraces built to hold tables remain to this day. In 1982, the Vietnam Veterans Memorial was constructed in the meadow at the western end of Constitution Gardens.

Constitution Gardens, looking southeast. The Washington Monument appears shrouded in scaffolding as part of a restoration that was completed in 2001.

Braddock's Rock may be Washington's answer to Plymouth Rock, but it hasn't received the same respect as the more famous stepping stone in Massachusetts. Buried and unburied over the years, today it lies at the bottom of a 37-foot well, alongside an approach ramp to the Roosevelt Bridge.

A large rock outcrop on the riverbank, Braddock's Rock was once a prominent landmark along the Potomac. The rock was said to have been the landing spot for General Edward Braddock and his troops on their way to Fort Duquesne (now Pittsburgh) in 1755, during the French and Indian War. A young George Washington, then serving as Braddock's aide-de-camp, was presumably present as well. Braddock planned to capture the fort from the French, but instead, his force was soundly defeated. Braddock himself was mortally wounded.

Today, it seems doubtful that Braddock ever set foot on the rock. It was, however, used by surveyors as a landmark in numerous early surveys, and the rock bore a metal tag stamped with the legend "Key of All Keys." In the 1830s, when the Chesapeake and Ohio Canal was extended into Washington along the riverbank, part of Braddock's Rock was blasted away.

When the Army Corps of Engineers filled the mud flats in the river at the end of the nineteenth century, the ground was raised, leaving the rock at the bottom of a hole. The attorney general asked that the important benchmark on the rock be preserved, and the hole was lined with a brick wall.

In 1919, a naval hospital was built over the site, and the rock would not see the light of day until the hospital was demolished in 1949. In the 1950s, the rock was visible at the bottom of a hole in a parking lot, surrounded by a fence. When the Theodore Roosevelt Bridge was built, the westbound approach ramp from Constitution Avenue was deflected slightly to avoid the rock. The grade was raised again, and a 37-foot well was built around the rock. There it remains today, marked with a plaque, installed when the bridge was completed in 1964.

Top. Braddock's Rock as it appeared at the end of the nineteenth century, between an extension of the C&O Canal and the wall of the old Naval Observatory.

Bottom. Braddock's Rock lies at the bottom of this 37-foot well, alongside a westbound approach ramp to the Theodore Roosevelt Bridge, 200 feet west of Twenty-Third Street.

Abraham Lincoln (1809–1865), 16th president of the United States, guided the nation through the Civil War, preserved the Union, and freed the slaves. His dramatic rise from humble origins; his tragic death; and his honesty, sound judgment, and freedom from bitterness and prejudice all contributed to his reputation.

This memorial to Lincoln, constructed between 1914 and 1922, is in the form of a classical temple, combining elements of Greek and Roman architecture. Commensurate with the magnitude of Lincoln's reputation and his role in American history, the memorial occupies a site equal in importance to that of the Washington Monument.

The general design of the Lincoln Memorial dates to 1902, when the McMillan Commission presented to Congress its vastly influential plan for the improvement of Washington's parks. (A rendering is reproduced below.) At the time, the site of the Lincoln Memorial and the reflecting pool was newly made land, still covered with weeds and brush. The McMillan Commission pro-posed completing the unfinished park by extending the Mall westward to the Potomac, where the memorial to Lincoln would terminate its long axis.

The commission comprised four members, but the Lincoln Memorial and the reflecting pool were largely the work of architect Charles McKim. He envisioned the memorial as an open group of columns, surrounded by a traffic circle with tree-lined avenues radiating outward, similar to the Arc de Triomphe in Paris. A bronze statue of Lincoln would stand in front of the colonnade.

Construction of the memorial was set in motion in 1911, when Congress created the Lincoln Memorial Commission and charged it with selecting a site, an architect, and a design. Ultimately, the commission chose the present site on the Potomac, as recommended by the McMillan Commission. Architects Henry Bacon and John Russell Pope (who later designed the Jefferson Memorial and the National Gallery of Art) each submitted designs, and Bacon's scheme was accepted in 1912.

Bacon's plan called for a Doric temple similar to the Parthenon in Athens, with the long side facing the Mall. Instead of a Greek-style pediment, he proposed a Roman-style attic. A statue of Lincoln would be ensconced in a large room in the interior. Bacon specialized in designing monuments and memorials, although his work is not well represented in Washington. He was a protégé of Charles McKim, so it is not surprising that his design was basically similar to that proposed by McKim in 1902.

Work on the foundations began in 1914. Steel tubes were driven to bedrock, about 50 feet below the surface, and filled with concrete. An upper foundation was made of reinforced concrete. The superstructure, built entirely of stone, was begun in 1915 and completed in 1917. In the following years, the interior, terraces, and approaches were completed. The memorial opened to the public in

The Lincoln Memorial and the reflecting pool were first proposed by the McMillan Commission in 1902. In this rendering that accompanied the commission's plans, the colonnade appears open with a standing figure of Lincoln in front, details that were later changed.

ABOVE. A special rail line leading from the B&O Railroad in Georgetown carried the enormous blocks of marble to the site.

LEFT. The Lincoln Memorial under construction, c. 1917.

RIGHT. The statue of Abraham Lincoln with sculptor Daniel Chester French (left) and Henry Bacon, architect of the Lincoln Memorial, 1922.

CLOCKWISE (from top left):

Boy Scouts holding a semaphore contest at the Rainbow Pool shortly after its completion in 1922.

Martin Luther King Jr. delivered his "I Have a Dream" speech from the steps of the Lincoln Memorial on August 28, 1963. The memorial to the Great Emancipator was a potent symbol for the Civil Rights movement, and King's speech was the climax of the March on Washington for Jobs and Freedom. King is seen here being interviewed inside the Lincoln Memorial on the day of his speech.

On Easter Sunday 1939, renowned contralto Marian Anderson sang before a crowd of 75,000 on the steps of the Lincoln Memorial. Anderson had been denied the use of Constitution Hall by the Daughters of the American Revolution because of her race. First Lady Eleanor Roosevelt arranged for her to sing at the Lincoln Memorial instead, and the concert was broadcast on national radio. Anderson's performance remains one of the defining moments of the Civil Rights movement.

June 1921, and the dedication was held on Memorial Day 1922. The reflecting pool was completed soon thereafter.

The exterior is constructed of an ultra-white marble from Colorado. There are 36 Doric columns, 44 feet in height—one for each state in the Union at the time of Lincoln's death. Above each column is the name of a state. Inside the entrance are two additional columns. On the attic wall are the names of each of the 48 states in the Union when the memorial was completed.

The columns tilt inward slightly, an architectural "refinement," first used in ancient Greece, that lends the memorial an appearance of geometrical perfection. The exterior walls are tilted inward to a lesser degree.

Architect Bacon and the Lincoln Memorial Commission selected Daniel Chester French, the most highly regarded American sculptor of his day, and Bacon's personal friend, to create the statue of Lincoln. French was commissioned in December 1915, but he had already set to work on a series of models. Although the statue was originally planned to be about 10 feet in height, when Bacon and French placed a full-sized model in the atrium, it was dwarfed by the monument's Herculean proportions. With enlarged photographs, they determined that 19 feet would be the proper height.

French provided a scale model to a stone-carving firm, which cut the statue from 28 blocks of white marble from Georgia. The cutting began in 1918, and assembly of the statue was completed in 1920.

*Abraham Lincoln* is French's masterwork and is probably the best-known sculpture by any American artist. Lincoln is sitting in a large chair, his body relaxed. His face and hands express his intensity, strength, and dedication to purpose. Draped over the chair is an American flag. The entire work radiates a weighty majesty.

The statue is situated against the center of the west wall in a large room, which is divided into three parts by two rows of Ionic columns made of Indiana limestone. The walls are the same material; the floor is pink Tennessee marble. The room is lit from above by a skylight with translucent marble panels in a bronze frame, supplemented by electric lights. Lincoln's "Gettysburg Address" is carved into the south wall; above it is *Emancipation*, a mural by Jules Guérin. On the north wall is *Reunion*, also by Guérin, and Lincoln's "Second Inaugural Address."

The reflecting pool in front of the memorial was originally designed to be cruciform, but some wartime temporary buildings then facing Constitution Avenue were in the way, and the pool was built as a rectangle instead. To its east is the smaller Rainbow Pool, so named because an array of water jets, activated on special occasions, created a rainbow effect. In 2001, the Rainbow Pool was demolished to make way for the National World War II Memorial. The pool was reconstructed, in modified form, and incorporated into the new memorial.

The Lincoln Memorial, seen here in 1961, is architect Henry Bacon's masterpiece, one of the finest examples of classical architecture in Washington and a fitting tribute to Lincoln's memory.

In 1931, the western approaches to the Lincoln Memorial were nearing completion. From the right are Memorial Bridge, the Water Gate steps, and the Rock Creek Parkway.

The Arlington Memorial Bridge crosses the Potomac River, symbolically reuniting the North and South, bitter foes in the Civil War. At one end of the bridge is the shrine to Abraham Lincoln, the savior of the Union. At the other end is Arlington, once the estate of Robert E. Lee, commander of the Confederate armies, and now the site of Arlington National Cemetery.

After the Civil War, Congress considered various plans for a bridge to memorialize American valor in the war. The favored site linked New York Avenue with Arlington Cemetery at the approximate location of today's Roosevelt Bridge. In 1902, the influential McMillan Commission, citing these plans, recommended a bridge that would form an ensemble with the proposed Lincoln Memorial and Water

Gate. The commission urged that the bridge be low above the river and simple in design so as not to compete with the memorial.

The impetus for constructing the bridge is said to have come on Armistice Day 1921, when President Warren Harding spent one and a half hours stranded in traffic on his way to a ceremony at the Tomb of the Unknown Soldier. The following year, Congress created the Arlington Memorial Bridge Commission, which selected the firm of McKim, Mead and White to design the bridge. The architect was William Kendall.

Work on the bridge began in 1926 and was completed by 1932. It is 2,138 feet long and made of reinforced concrete covered with granite. There is a steel draw span in the center, painted to match the stone, but it has not been opened for many years.

Adjacent to the bridge is the Water Gate, 48 granite steps that lead from the river to the circle around the Lincoln Memorial. In 1902, the McMillan Commission proposed the Water Gate as a ceremonial gateway to the city from the river. In the 1920s, as planning was underway for the Memorial Bridge, an argument was made against constructing the steps: In the McMillan Plan, the Lincoln Memorial was to have been an open group of columns, similar to the Brandenburg Gate in Berlin. Since the memorial was built as an enclosed structure, it couldn't be entered from the side facing the river, and the steps made little sense. The steps were built anyway and completed in 1931. However, they are bisected by Ohio Drive, which was routed just above the river to keep heavy traffic off the circle. In later years, the Water Gate lent its name first to a restaurant that stood on the site of the Kennedy Center and then to the famous apartment, office, and hotel complex in Foggy Bottom. The steps are little used today.

At the Washington end of the bridge are two equestrian statues by Leo Friedlander, *The Arts of War*. Nearby, at the entrance to the Rock Creek and Potomac Parkway, are *The Arts of Peace*, two similar works by James Earle Fraser. The four sculptures were dedicated in 1951. They were originally intended to be carved from granite, but were instead made of gilded bronze, a gift from the Italian government after World War II.

ABOVE. *The Arts of Peace*, two gilded bronze sculptures by James Earle Fraser, flank the entrance to the Rock Creek and Potomac Parkway. Here, on the south, is *Aspiration and Literature*.

TOP LEFT. Between 1935 and 1973, concerts were held on summer nights at the Water Gate (the steps in the foreground), seen here in 1942. The National Symphony Orchestra and others performed in a bandshell floating on a barge, while concertgoers sat on the steps or in canoes on the water. To the left is the Memorial Bridge.

BOTTOM LEFT. The Water Gate barge being towed through the open draw span of the Memorial Bridge, 1952.

LEFT. Opening day at the Speedway, October 19, 1903. A parade of carriages more than a mile long marked the completion of Seventeenth Street across the Mall and the first segment of the Speedway, which bordered the Tidal Basin.

RIGHT. Water flows in one direction through the Tidal Basin, controlled by gates in the bridges, to keep the Washington Channel free of silt.

Most visitors to Washington are unaware that a large portion of the Mall was constructed on "made" land. Until the 1880s, the sites of the Lincoln Memorial, the reflecting pool, and the Jefferson Memorial lay in the Potomac River.

Beginning work in 1882, the Army Corps of Engineers added 628 acres of new land to Washington by dredging the Potomac and dumping the silt along the Washington shore. The dredging was a practical matter: It cleared the river channel for navigation and filled the noxious Potomac Flats.

The flats extended almost to the base of the Washington Monument, less than one-half mile from the White House. Raw sewage, poured into the Potomac daily, accumulated on the mud flats, which were exposed at low tide. The stench was abominable, and the flats were considered a breeding ground for disease.

The work of clearing the channel was accomplished with floating dredges. Enormous steam-driven pumps sucked silt off the river bottom and pumped it through 20-inch pipes floating on pontoons. The pipes, up to a mile long, deposited the fill in the desired location, where it was contained by barriers.

In 1897, Congress combined this new land with about 100 acres of existing land to form Potomac Park. Generally speaking, Potomac Park includes the area south and west of the Washington Monument, encompassing the site of the Lincoln Memorial and the reflecting pool, the Tidal Basin, and an artificial island southeast of the Tidal Basin that ends at Hains Point.

The location of the new shoreline appears to have been laid out by the Corps of Engineers based on practical, rather than aesthetic, considerations. Most of the work was already done when the McMillan Commission presented its influential 1902 plan for the development of Washington's parks. The commission suggested formal landscaping for the Lincoln Memorial and the Tidal Basin and an informal treatment for East Potomac Park, but it only sketched the broad outlines of the plan. The details were left to the Corps of Engineers.

It was a park in name only, however, being mostly muck covered with weeds, brush, and willows. In 1902, work began on improvements. Roads were built; trees, planted; and grass, seeded. The work was carried out by the Office of Public Buildings and Grounds, a division of the Army Corps of Engineers.

Seventeenth Street was cut through the Mall in 1902. Within a few years, roads were built around the perimeter of the Tidal Basin, out to Hains Point and back, and along the Potomac from the Tidal Basin inlet to Twenty-Sixth Street, N.W. Collectively, the roads were known as the Speedway, as drivers could "speed" in their carriages and automobiles. For a while, Saturday after-noons were set aside for this purpose. The Speedway still exists in modified form—the portion along the Potomac and the Washington Channel is known as Ohio Drive.

In 1908, the Army Corps of Engineers raised the site of the Lincoln Memorial to its present grade with landfill and filled the sewer canal. In 1909, B Street North (later Constitution Avenue) was extended westward to meet the new road along the river. Landfill in West Potomac Park was completed that same year.

During World War II, Independence Avenue was extended west through Potomac Park from Fourteenth Street to the Lincoln Memorial, necessitating a short bridge over the Tidal Basin. The extension was intended to improve access to the Pentagon and other new federal buildings in Virginia.

The sewer canal in Potomac Park was not one of Washington's signal attractions, and photographs of it are correspondingly rare. The canal carried raw sewage from an outlet near the lockhouse on Constitution Avenue, through Potomac Park, to the river. This photograph was probably taken in 1908 as the canal was being filled in. On the left, silt pumped from the river channel flows from a pipe into the canal. In the foreground is a bridge that temporarily carried a riverside carriage path over the mouth of the canal. In the 1920s, the John Ericsson Memorial would be erected not far from this spot.

**JOHN PAUL JONES MEMORIAL.** The greatest American naval hero of the Revolutionary War, John Paul Jones (1747–1792) is generally regarded as the father of the U.S. Navy, in spirit if not in actual fact. Jones was first commissioned into the tiny Continental navy in 1775. He commanded a number of vessels in succession, raiding British shipping and capturing many prizes. As captain of the *Bonhomme Richard*, he captured the superior British warship *Serapis* in a dramatic battle in the North Sea. During the fierce engagement, Captain Richard Pearson of the *Serapis* asked if Jones was ready to surrender. Engraved on the memorial is Jones's famous reply: "Surrender? I have not yet begun to fight!"

Jones died in Paris in 1792 and was buried in an unmarked grave. In 1905, after a long search by the American ambassador, his body was found and returned to the United States for burial at the Naval Academy at Annapolis, Maryland. Shortly thereafter, Congress appropriated funds for this memorial, now located at the terminus of Seventeenth Street on the Tidal Basin. The memorial was unveiled in 1912, the first monument in Potomac Park. Jones is depicted in a 10-foot-high bronze statue, the work of sculptor Charles H. Niehaus of New York. Jones appears resolute, as if regarding the progress of a battle; Niehaus intended Jones to appear as one who could accomplish anything he willed. Behind the statue is a classical marble pylon, 15 feet in height. On each side, water pours from the mouth of a stylized dolphin into a small pool. On the reverse side of the pylon is a bas-relief of Jones raising the American flag on the *Bonhomme Richard*, said to be the first time the stars and stripes were flown on an American warship.

**DISTRICT OF COLUMBIA WORLD WAR MEMORIAL.** This 47-foot-tall Doric temple is located in the woods east of the Korean War Veterans Memorial, between the reflecting pool and Independence Avenue. Dedicated in 1931, it honors the men and women of the District of Columbia who served in World War I. Inscribed on the base are the names of 500 District residents killed in the war, while the names of 26,000 who served are recorded inside the cornerstone. The memorial was made of white marble from Danby, Vermont, and replaced a wooden bandstand that was erected in West Potomac Park near the Inlet Bridge in 1909. Forty-four feet in diameter, the memorial is large enough to accommodate an 80-piece band, but is not used for this purpose today. The architects were Frederick H. Brooke, of Washington, and his associates Nathan Wyeth and Horace W. Peaslee.

TOP. The John Paul Jones Memorial, c. 1912, shows the Scottish-born Revolutionary War naval hero in full military dress, his left hand clutching the pommel of his sword.

LEFT. On each side of the John Paul Jones Memorial, water spews from the mouth of a stylized dolphin.

RIGHT. The District of Columbia World War Memorial.

**John Ericsson Memorial.** John Ericsson (1803–1889) was a Swedish-born naval engineer who emigrated to the United States in 1839. During the Civil War, he designed and supervised the construction of the ironclad *Monitor* for the Union navy, a ship that revolutionized naval warfare. As an inventor, he is best known for perfecting the screw propeller.

This memorial to Ericsson is 820 feet south of the Lincoln Memorial, overlooking the Potomac River. Ericsson appears as a seated figure, seemingly deep in thought. Behind the figure is the tree Yggdrasill, which, in Norse mythology, binds together the universe with its roots and branches. Three allegorical figures represent Ericsson's principal qualities: Vision, a woman peering into the distance; Adventure, a Norse warrior; and Labor, an American iron worker. The decoration on the base is Norse in inspiration.

The memorial was the work of sculptor James Earle Fraser. Best known as the designer of the American buffalo nickel, Fraser was responsible for *The Arts of Peace* (see page 109) and many other works of public sculpture in Washington. Congress authorized the Ericsson Memorial in 1916, and Swedish societies in America raised $25,000, almost half of the cost; Congress appropriated the remainder. Working from a full-sized plaster model provided by Fraser, a stone-cutting firm carved the allegorical figures on site from a 40-ton block of pink granite. The figure of Ericsson was carved from a second, 25-ton block.

When it was clear that the memorial would not be completed in time for its unveiling in 1926, the granite blocks were moved aside and replaced with the plaster model, painted pink to resemble stone. The ceremony could not be postponed because it was planned to coincide with a visit by Crown Prince Gustaf Adolf of Sweden. At the unveiling, held May 29, 1926, the crown princess pulled a cord, revealing the memorial to the crowd, accompanied by a 21-gun salute from a naval ship anchored in the Potomac. This was immediately followed by an address by President Calvin Coolidge. The memorial was completed a year later, in October 1927.

Top. The John Ericsson Memorial, c. 1930, was financed in part by Americans of Swedish ancestry.

Bottom. On May 15, 1918, the world's first regularly scheduled airmail service was launched from the lawn in West Potomac Park, connecting Washington with Philadelphia and New York. Today, a plaque marks the spot by the Potomac River near the FDR Memorial.

GEORGE MASON MEMORIAL. George Mason (1725–1792) was a planter and patriot from nearby Fairfax County, Virginia, and an associate of George Washington and Thomas Jefferson. In 1776, he wrote the Virginia Declaration of Rights, which served as the basis for the Bill of Rights in the U.S. Constitution. Later, Mason famously earned the ire of Washington by refusing to sign the Constitution, largely because he feared a strong central government. Mason objected that the document lacked a bill of rights, which was added in 1791, a year before his death.

The George Mason Memorial is located in West Potomac Park, to the southwest of the Jefferson Memorial. It was dedicated in 2002. The memorial features a larger-than-life-sized statue of George Mason by sculptor Wendy Ross of Bethesda, Maryland. Mason appears sitting on a bench under a broad trellis, flanked by inscriptions bearing selections from his writings. The only known life portrait of Mason was destroyed in a fire, so his appearance here is somewhat conjectural. Ross relied on written descriptions by contemporaries and on the facial features of some of Mason's descendants. Mason's figure appears with a volume of Cicero in hand, as if pausing for a moment of reflection.

The memorial and the landscaping were designed by the firm Rhodeside & Harwell of Alexandria, Virginia. It was sponsored by the board of regents of Gunston Hall, Mason's plantation in Fairfax County, Virginia. Appropriately, the memorial abuts the George Mason Memorial Bridge, the westernmost span of the Fourteenth Street Bridge.

CUBAN FRIENDSHIP URN. This marble urn commemorates the friendship between the peoples of Cuba and the United States. It was originally installed in a rose garden between the Jefferson Memorial and the Potomac River, until construction of the first of three spans of the Fourteenth Street Bridge forced its removal in 1947. The urn was believed lost until 1996, when it was rediscovered in a National Park Service storage yard. It was restored and reinstalled beside the Fourteenth Street Bridge in 1997, near the original site. The urn was rededicated in June 1998.

President Calvin Coolidge received the urn as a gift during a visit to Cuba in 1928. On the reverse side is a bas-relief sculpture of the sinking of the battleship U.S.S. *Maine* in Havana harbor in 1898. A mysterious explosion destroyed the ship and killed 266 of the men on board, leading to war between the United States and Spain and, ultimately, to Cuban independence. The urn was made of marble from a monument to the *Maine* that stood in Havana, before a hurricane destroyed it in 1926.

LEFT. The George Mason Memorial features an outstanding work of figurative sculpture by Wendy Ross.

RIGHT. After 50 years in storage, the Cuban Friendship Urn was restored to Potomac Park in 1997.

Franklin Delano Roosevelt (1882–1945) guided the nation through the most difficult years of the twentieth century. First elected president in 1932, he tackled the Great Depression in his first two terms in office and, in his third, marshaled Allied forces to defeat the Axis powers in World War II. He died in April 1945, shortly into his fourth term.

The Franklin Delano Roosevelt Memorial stretches 800 feet along the south side of the Tidal Basin and covers about 7½ acres. The memorial narrates the story of Roosevelt's 12 years in office with granite walls, sculpture, waterfalls, and inscriptions, arranged in four rooms corresponding to the four terms of his presidency. It is a pleasant place to visit as well, with six waterfalls, carefully chosen plantings, and beautiful views of the Tidal Basin and the Washington Monument. There are nine bronze sculptures by five American artists: Leonard Baskin, Neil Estern, Robert Graham, Tom Hardy, and George Segal. The memorial itself was designed by Lawrence Halprin, a landscape architect from California.

The memorial was realized only after a gestation period of more than five decades. The Franklin Delano Roosevelt Memorial Commission was first authorized by Congress in 1946, but was not formed until 1955. The commission selected the Tidal Basin site in 1957 and held the first design competition in 1960. The winning

entry had a circle of massive (up to 165 feet tall) concrete steles bearing quotations from FDR, but the commission later dropped the plan due to public objections. A second competition, held in 1966, was awarded to prominent architect Marcel Breuer for an immense granite pinwheel centered on a granite cube. Breuer's design was rejected by the Commission of Fine Arts (CFA) for a perceived lack of artistic merit.

A third competition, held in 1974, went to Halprin, whose winning design was less controversial because it harmonized with the bucolic setting along the Tidal Basin. It was approved by the CFA (after being reduced in scale), but languished for another decade because of a lack of funding. Finally, in 1989, Congress appropriated funds for the memorial's construction, and work began in 1994. It was dedicated on May 2, 1997.

The memorial soon became the subject of controversy over its depiction of Roosevelt's paralysis, the legacy of a 1921 bout with polio. During his lifetime, Roosevelt strove to hide his disability, but more recently his triumph over this handicap has made him a symbol for many disabled Americans. Under pressure from advocates for the disabled, Congress authorized the addition of a statue of FDR in a wheelchair, shortly after the memorial's completion. The new statue, the work of sculptor Robert Graham, was placed in an addition to the front of the memorial. It was unveiled in 2001.

Top. The memorial comprises four open rooms. The second room is dedicated to FDR's second term in office (1937–1941), when his New Deal, an array of federal programs designed to revitalize the economy and provide relief from the Depression, went into high gear. On the left are *The Rural Couple* and *The Breadline*, by sculptor George Segal, of New Brunswick, New Jersey. In the alcove to the right is *Fireside Chat*, also by Segal.

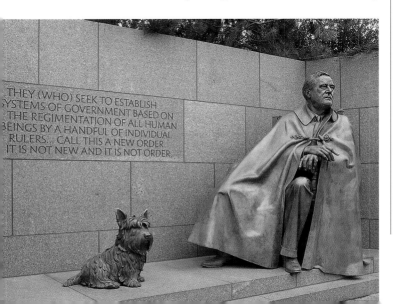

Left. In the *Third-Term Room*, dedicated to the war years (1941–1945), is this statue of FDR and his Scottish Terrier, Fala, by sculptor Neil Estern, of Brooklyn, New York.

Dating from the end of the nineteenth century, the Tidal Basin was created when the Army Corps of Engineers filled the surrounding mud flats and dredged the basin to a depth of eight feet. Work on the 111-acre basin reportedly uncovered numerous wrecks, some predating the establishment of Washington in 1791.

The basin is famous for the hundreds of cherry trees that burst with magnificent blossoms each spring, but it was created for a more prosaic purpose: to flush silt from the Washington Channel. The rising tide flows into the Tidal Basin through the Inlet Bridge, then out to the channel through the Outlet Bridge. One-way gates in the bridges ensure that the water flows in the proper direction.

Between 1918 and 1925, there was a popular bathing beach on the Tidal Basin at the present site of the Jefferson Memorial. The beach was about 1,600 feet long and served thousands of swimmers daily during the hot summer months. In those days recreational facilities in Washington were segregated, and the beach was strictly reserved for whites.

In 1925 the Army Corps of Engineers started work on a similar beach across the Tidal Basin for blacks. Debate in Congress followed; several members believed that the existing beach was an eyesore that detracted from the beauty of Potomac Park, and there were arguments over whether the basin was unsanitary. As a result, the beach for whites was closed the same year, and work on the new beach ceased. Today, it is illegal to swim in the Tidal Basin and in the Potomac River, although it is generally safe from a health standpoint.

The first of the famous cherry trees that ring the Tidal Basin were a gift from the City of Tokyo. Unfortunately, the initial shipment from Japan in 1910 was infested with insects and had to be burned. A second shipment of 3,020 trees arrived in 1912. In a ceremony that same year, First Lady Helen Taft and Viscountess Chinda, wife of the Japanese ambassador, planted the first two trees. Located north of the Tidal Basin, these two trees still survive and are marked with a plaque. Overall, about 150 of the original trees remain.

Today, there are approximately 1,700 cherry trees around the Tidal Basin. The vast majority are of the Yoshino variety, which is quite popular in Japan. There are another 1,700 trees in East Potomac Park, and about 350 are on the grounds of the Washington Monument. The cherry trees bloom between mid-March and mid-April, but the blossoms last only a few days. They form a spectacular display, and hundreds of thousands of visitors come to the Tidal Basin every year during the peak period. An annual Cherry Blossom Festival has been held since 1935, highlighted by a parade on Constitution Avenue. The timing of the peak period for the blooms cannot be predicted in advance and doesn't necessarily coincide with the festival.

The Tidal Basin with the cherry trees in full bloom.

Clockwise (from top left):

The Inlet Bridge, c. 1910, was built between 1888 and 1889.

A bathing beach was located on the site of the Jefferson Memorial on the Tidal Basin between 1918 and 1925.

A diving platform at the bathing beach.

Contestants at a beauty contest held at the beach, c. 1922. Women's bathing suits had to extend within three inches of the knees, and openings below the arms were not permitted.

The Outlet Bridge under construction. It was built between 1908 and 1910.

Thomas Jefferson (1743–1826) composed an epitaph for his own tomb, listing what he considered to be his three greatest accomplishments: "Author of the Declaration of American Independence, of the Statute of Virginia for Religious Freedom, and Father of the University of Virginia."

Jefferson, a scientist and architect as well as a statesman, failed to mention that he had also served as third president of the United States. After his death on July 4, 1826, Jefferson's reputation grew slowly. It would be more than a century before he was honored with this memorial, dedicated in 1943.

In its 1902 plan for the Mall, the McMillan Commission suggested the Tidal Basin as the site for a great monument to an unspecified person. The proposed monument would terminate the cross axis of the Mall, an imaginary north–south line connecting the Tidal Basin site with the grounds of the Washington Monument and the White House.

In the 1920s, a monument to President Theodore Roosevelt was planned for this important site, and a design by John Russell Pope was selected. Pope's scheme had two semicircular arrays of columns surrounding a large fountain, but Congress never funded its construction.

Franklin Delano Roosevelt, a Democrat first elected president in 1932, was a great admirer of Jefferson and his interest led to the establishment of the Jefferson Memorial. It helped that the Democrats, who had come to see Jefferson as the father of their party, now controlled Congress as well.

Congress created the Thomas Jefferson Memorial Commission in 1934 to plan and construct an appropriate monument. Citing Jefferson's interest in classical architecture, the commission decided that the memorial should be classical in style and hired John Russell Pope, the preeminent American classical architect. The commission favored the Tidal Basin as the only suitably important site left on the Mall.

Pope devised plans for the Tidal Basin and three alternative sites. His scheme for the Tidal Basin, resembling the one in the McMillan Plan, had a colossal open pantheon with a statue of Jefferson inside, while the basin would have been reshaped into a rectangle. The commission favored this option, but asked Pope to scale it down, since it would have been far too costly to build.

In December 1936, Pope returned to the memorial commission with two designs. The commission accepted Scheme A (see the rendering on this page), but when it presented the plan to the Commission of Fine Arts (CFA) the following March, it was rejected. Since 1910, all additions to the Mall must be submitted to the CFA, which principally comprises artists and architects appointed by the president. The CFA was unhappy that there had been no competition; it believed that Pope's design was an unimaginative recycling of an ancient building and too similar to the Lincoln Memorial. Furthermore, Pope's plan would require destroying nearly all of the cherry trees on the Tidal Basin.

Pope's scheme, once made public, was savaged by a vast array of prominent architects and critics. Beaux-Arts classicism, at its height when the McMillan Commission presented its plan for the Mall in 1902, had now passed out of fashion. Modernism had taken its place, but Pope believed in readapting a few ancient prototypes, rather than radical innovation. Critics called his design for the Jefferson Memorial pompous and uninspired, "applied archeology" that didn't capture Jefferson's spirit or imagination. Some criticized its similarity to the National Gallery of Art, also designed by Pope and based on the Roman Pantheon.

TOP. John Russell Pope (1874–1937), of New York City, designed the Jefferson Memorial, as well as the National Gallery of Art and several other important Washington buildings. He was the most prominent classical architect of his day.

BOTTOM. Scheme A for the Jefferson Memorial, the first shown to the public, would have radically reshaped the Tidal Basin.

Pope died in August 1937, and his work was continued by two associates, Otto R. Eggers and Daniel P. Higgins, who produced some additional designs. The CFA preferred an adaptation of a scheme that Pope had created in the 1920s for the proposed memorial to Theodore Roosevelt, and the memorial commission agreed to accept it as a compromise, although it still preferred the pantheon.

Pope's widow, however, refused to grant permission to modify his work. In March 1938, the memorial commission reversed itself and went back to the pantheon design, claiming that it had not been aware that the modified Roosevelt Memorial design was in fact a rehash of an old design. The memorial commission submitted the pantheon to the CFA yet again—the Tidal Basin would be left intact—and again it was rejected. At the end of March, the memorial commission announced that it was going forward with the pantheon anyway, without CFA approval, and Congress provided funds to begin construction.

In September 1938 Frederick Law Olmsted Jr. was hired to plan the landscaping around the memorial, and in December, President Roosevelt presided over the groundbreaking ceremony. Protesters opposed destruction of the cherry trees on the site, but progress was only briefly delayed.

The foundations were constructed in 1939. The memorial was built on recent landfill, and piles were sunk to bedrock. The cornerstone was set in November 1939. Work continued in spite of World War II, and the memorial was completed in early 1942, when it was opened to the public. It is 184 feet in diameter. The exterior is made of white marble from Vermont, on a granite base. There are 54 Ionic columns; the 38 exterior columns are 41 feet high.

The rotunda is 92 feet tall. The walls are made of Georgia marble; the floor is pink Tennessee marble, and the interior of the dome is Indiana limestone. The room has four openings, each with

four columns. Between the openings are four panels with excerpts from Jefferson's writings.

The memorial was well underway before a sculptor for the Jefferson statue was selected. In July 1939, a jury selected six entrants from a field of 101 competitors. After several rounds of competition, sculptor Rudulph Evans of New York was chosen in October 1941.

The Thomas Jefferson Memorial was dedicated by President Roosevelt on April 13, 1943, the bicentennial of Jefferson's birth. The Declaration of Independence was on display in the memorial, guarded by four marines. Evans's sculpture of Jefferson was represented by a full-sized plaster cast painted to resemble bronze, since a wartime shortage of the metal (10,000 pounds were required) prevented casting of the statue.

The sculpture was completed after the war and installed in the rotunda in April 1947. It is 19 feet tall and stands on a black granite base. Jefferson is depicted in a relaxed posture, wearing a fur-trimmed coat and holding a scroll in one hand. The sculpture is said to be a good likeness, but it lacks the dynamism of Daniel Chester French's statue of Lincoln.

LEFT. The Thomas Jefferson Memorial, dedicated in 1943, is on the south side of the Tidal Basin. Its classical design, modeled on the Pantheon in Rome, was the subject of intense controversy.

RIGHT. The statue of Jefferson by Rudulph Evans was not installed in the rotunda until 1947, four years after the dedication of the memorial.

East Potomac Park looking north, c. 1925. The park is bordered by the Potomac River (left), the Tidal Basin (upper left), and the Washington Channel (right). In the foreground is Hains Point, named for Colonel Peter C. Hains, who supervised much of the dredging and filling that created the park.

East Potomac Park occupies about 330 acres of an artificial island southeast of the Tidal Basin. A public golf course fills about two-thirds of the park, and there are tennis courts, a swimming pool, a golf driving range, and a miniature golf course. The park is commonly known as Hains Point, after its southern tip, a popular destination for motorists. The railroad tracks just east of the Jefferson Memorial form the boundary with West Potomac Park.

The land occupied by East Potomac Park was created at the end of the nineteenth century when the U.S. Army Corps of Engineers dredged the Potomac River channel and deposited the silt behind barriers. The 1902 McMillan Plan recommended an informal treatment for the park, using natural river bottomlands as a model. The plan suggested a series of interconnected meadows, with a fringe of trees along the water.

Landfill operations in East Potomac Park were completed in 1911, and work began the following year on the landscaping. The Office of Public Buildings and Grounds, a division of the Army Corps of Engineers, built roads and planted trees, grass, and shrubs.

In 1916, the Corps of Engineers published a plan for the park that featured baseball diamonds and a golf course, which were soon constructed. Other aspects of the plan, including a boat harbor and a baseball stadium, were never implemented. Work on the golf course began in 1917. The first nine holes were opened to the public in 1920, and nine more opened in 1923. The park now has an 18-hole and two nine-hole golf courses that are very popular with District residents. Two identical colonnaded buildings, made of cast concrete, were finished about 1920, with changing rooms for men and women. They were intended to be wings of a larger building, but the center section that would have connected them was never built. Today, one of the buildings is a pro shop for golfers and a snack bar, while the other is a U.S. Park Police substation.

Nearby is a swimming pool, built in 1936 as a Public Works Administration project. There is also an 18-hole miniature golf course, which opened in 1931. It is believed to be the oldest continuously operating miniature golf course in the United States.

In response to the new popularity of automobile touring, a tourist camp was set up in the park in May 1921. Tents, cabins, showers, a commissary, a gas station, and other facilities were available. The camp served as an inexpensive alternative to

hotels until it closed in 1962. Offices for the National Capital Region of the National Park Service and a headquarters for the U.S. Park Police were built on the site between 1962 and 1963 and are still in use today.

Ohio Drive, which follows the perimeter of the park along the water, was built between 1912 and 1916. Together with roads in West Potomac Park, it was known as the Speedway, since park visitors could "speed" in their carriages and automobiles. Before home air-conditioning was popular, Washingtonians would spend hot summer nights sleeping in the park, where fresh breezes blew off the river.

Certainly the best-known landmark in East Potomac Park is *The Awakening*, a colossal statue of a bearded giant emerging from the earth. The work of J. Seward Johnson Jr., the cast-aluminum sculpture was installed at Hains Point in 1980, on long-term loan. Johnson, an heir to the Johnson and Johnson health products fortune, is best known for his realistic life-sized bronze sculptures of people engaged in everyday activities, which can be seen in parks and malls across the country. In 2000, Johnson donated *The Awakening* to a non-profit foundation. The group subsequently sold it to a real estate developer who plans to move it to Prince George's County, Maryland.

CLOCKWISE (from top left):

Between 1921 and 1962, there was a popular tourist camp in East Potomac Park, situated along the Potomac southeast of the railroad tracks.

*The Awakening*, by J. Seward Johnson Jr., at Hains Point.

The miniature golf course, seen here c. 1935, is still in operation.

HISTORY OF THE NATIONAL MALL:

1. L'Enfant quoted in Kite, *L'Enfant and Washington*, 48.
2. L'Enfant quoted in Kite, *L'Enfant and Washington*, 58.
3. Ellicott to the commissioners of the District of Columbia, January 4, 1793, Record Group 42, National Archives. Pamela Scott, personal communication.
4. McNeil, "Rock Creek Hundred." Priscilla W. McNeil, personal communication.
5. Hawkins, "The Landscape of the Federal City."
6. Hines, *Early Recollections of Washington City*, 67.
7. *Daily National Intelligencer*, October 4, 1804; October 17, 1804.
8. Hines, *Early Recollections of Washington City*, 83–84.
9. Thomas Twining quoted in Reps, *Washington on View*, 48.
10. Stephen Potter, personal communication.
11. Anonymous author quoted in John Clagett Proctor, "The Tragic Death of Andrew Jackson Downing and the Monument to His Memory," *Records of the Columbia Historical Society* 27 (1925): 250.
12. Bryan, *A History of the National Capital*, 24–25, 323.
13. Crouch, *The Eagle Aloft*, 346. Rhees, "Reminiscences of Ballooning," 261.
14. Allen, *History of the United States Capitol*, 342.
15. Keim, *Illustrated Hand-book*, 1874. U.S. Army Corps of Engineers, *Annual Report of the Chief of Engineers*, 1872.
16. Bowling, "From 'Federal Town' to 'National Capital.'"
17. U.S. Army Corps of Engineers, *Annual Report of the Chief of Engineers*, 1872–1877, 1912.
18. Ibid., 1875.
19. Ibid., 1872–1877.
20. Moore, *Charles Follen McKim*, 197.
21. Ibid., 198.
22. U.S. Senate, *The Improvement of the Park System of the District of Columbia*, 52.
23. McKim quoted in Moore, *Charles Follen McKim*, 302–303.
24. U.S. Commission of Fine Arts, Minutes, 1917–1922.
25. U.S. National Capital Park and Planning Commission, Minutes, October 20–21, 1933.
26. Public Law 70–1036.
27. "Mall Development Seen in Relocating of Botanic Garden," *Washington Post*, December 22, 1926.
28. "Ickes Removal of Mall Trees Flayed in House," *Washington Post*, May 15, 1935.
29. "Work on Million-Dollar Mall Now Is 90 Per Cent Completed," *Washington Post*, October 4, 1936. "New Capital Mall Near Completion," *New York Times*, October 4, 1936. Vertical file, Washingtoniana Division, D.C. Public Library.

30. "Compromise Offered States Requesting Names on Mall," *Washington Post*, July 31, 1937. "Veto Kills Plan to Name Roads After 4 States," *Washington Post*, August 28, 1937.
31. "The New 'Avenue of the States,'" *Washington Post*, June 23, 1929; the plan appeared in the 1930 annual report of the National Capital Park and Planning Commission.
32. "Vast Federal Office Plan Weighed," *Washington Post*, April 18, 1941.
33. "Planners Map Less Jammed, Statelier D.C.," *Washington Post*, September 21, 1941.
34. J. Carter Brown, "The Mall and the Commission of Fine Arts," in Longstreth, *The Mall in Washington, 1791–1991*, 249–261. John M. Woodbridge, personal communication. Vertical file, Washingtoniana Division, D.C. Public Library.
35. Wolf Von Eckardt, "Rows of Trees on a Green Expanse," *Washington Post*, December 15, 1973.
36. Public Law 99–652.
37. Public Law 108–126.
38. Public Law 108–108.
39. U.S. Senate, *The Improvement of the Park System of the District of Columbia*, 45.

U.S. BOTANIC GARDEN: Act of May 15, 1850, ch. 10, 9 *Stat*. 427. U.S. Army Corps of Engineers, *Annual Report of the Chief of Engineers*, 1868, 1869, 1871. U.S. Congress, House of Representatives, *Letter from the Commissioner of Public Buildings Transmitting His Annual Report for 1850*, 31st Cong., 2nd Sess., 1851, H. Doc. 47. *Daily National Intelligencer*, December 11, 1848. *Daily National Intelligencer*, November 6, 1850. Keim, *Illustrated Hand-book*, 1874. Rathbun, *The Columbian Institute*, 51–54. "Our Botanic Garden," *Washington Post*, April 4, 1934.

WASHINGTON CANAL: U.S. House of Representatives, *Investigation Into the Affairs of the District of Columbia*, 114–124, 147–149, 597–600.

TIBER CREEK: Keim, *Illustrated Hand-book*, 1874. "Floods in Washington, D.C." scrapbooks, Washingtoniana Division, D.C. Public Library.

MISSOURI AND MAINE AVENUES: Act of May 7, 1822, ch. 96, 3 *Stat*. 691.

GEORGE WASHINGTON MEMORIAL BUILDING: U. S. Grant III, *Annual Report of the Director of Public Buildings and Public Parks of the National Capital*, Washington, D.C.: Government Printing Office, 1926. Vertical file, Washingtoniana Division, D.C. Public Library.

HIRSHHORN MUSEUM AND SCULPTURE GARDEN: Grace Glueck, "Hirshhorn Museum Unveiled in Capital," *New York Times*, October 2, 1974. Paul Goldberger, "A Fortress of a Building that Works as a Museum," *New York Times*, October 2, 1974. Hilton Kramer, "A Collection that Puts Museum in Select Class," *New York Times*, October 2, 1974.

CONSTITUTION AVENUE: Vertical file, Washingtoniana Division, D.C. Public Library. U.S. Army Corps of Engineers, *Annual Report of the Chief of Engineers*, 1874. "Local News," *Evening Star*, November 3, 1873. "Old Capitol Gateposts," *Evening Star*, September 21, 1913.

BALTIMORE AND POTOMAC RAILROAD STATION: "Landmark Being Removed: Old Pennsylvania Railroad Station Soon Will be Demolished," *Washington Post*, August 16, 1908.

FISH COMMISSION: Keim, *Illustrated Hand-book*, 1888. "To Lose Beauty Spot: 'Government Fish Ponds' Will Be Abandoned," *Evening Star*, March 30, 1907. "Bathing Beach Open: Boys Have Great Time and Make Much Noise," *Evening Star*, July 1, 1910. Act of March 3, 1855, ch. 175, 10 *Stat*. 665. U.S. Congress, House of Representatives, *Report of the Secretary of War*, 35th Cong., 1st Sess., 1857, H. Doc. 2. Rathbun, *The United States National Museum*, 236–238. Jack Eisen, "Historic Landmark Being Razed in Southwest," *Washington Post*, January 19, 1964.

DEPARTMENT OF AGRICULTURE: Keim, *Illustrated Hand-book*, 1874. "Great Floral Show," *Evening Star*, October 31, 1904. "Old Tree House Put in Storage: Famous Redwood Temporarily at Arlington Farm," *Evening Star*, January 18, 1932. "30,000 Plants are Transferred to Greenbelt, Mall Greenhouses are Being Wrecked," *Washington Post*, March 6, 1940. "Bids to be Opened on Tempos Removal," *Evening Star*, May 9, 1958. U.S. Army Corps of Engineers, *Annual Report of the Chief of Engineers*, 1887.

WASHINGTON MONUMENT: Keim, *Illustrated Hand-book*, 1888. "Laying the Corner-stone of the Monument to Washington," *Daily National Intelligencer*, July 6, 1848.

PROPAGATING GARDEN: Rathbun, *The Columbian Institute*, 53. U.S. Army Corps of Engineers, *Annual Report of the Chief of Engineers*, 1874. Keim, *Illustrated Hand-book*, 1874. Heine, *National Capital Parks*, 44–46. Robert J. Lewis, "Tidal Basin Buildings' Razing is Under Way: 20 Park Service Utility Structures in West Potomac Park Will Go," *Evening Star*, August 25, 1962.

National World War II Memorial: Benjamin Forgey, "The Return of the Rainbow: Restoring a Fountain on the Mall," *Washington Post*, May 14, 1988.

Wartime Temporary Buildings: Vertical file, Washingtoniana Division, D.C. Public Library.

Constitution Gardens: Wolf Von Eckardt, "The Slow Greening of the Mall," *Washington Post*, July 27, 1974. Keith Butler, "Mall Park Construction Set This Week," *Washington Post*, July 23, 1974. Paul Hodge, "Constitution Gardens: A Bicentennial Gift to Us," *Washington Post*, May 28, 1976.

Braddock's Rock: Vertical file, Washingtoniana Division, D.C. Public Library.

Arlington Memorial Bridge and the Water Gate: Library of Congress Lot 12013-rri vertical file on the Water Gate Barge.

Potomac Park: "President Speeds Letter by Air Mail: Places Communication in Bag at Initial Flight from District," *Evening Star*, May 15, 1918.

John Paul Jones Memorial: "Memorials and Monuments" scrapbooks, Washingtoniana Division, D.C. Public Library. "Honored by Nation: Statue Unveiled to Memory of John Paul Jones," *Evening Star*, April 17, 1912.

District of Columbia World War Memorial: "Hoover Appeals for World Peace at Dedication of D.C. War Memorial," *Evening Star*, November 11, 1931. "Temple Contract Given Baird Co.: War Memorial of Danby Marble to be Reared Near Reflecting Pool," *Evening Star*, April 4, 1931.

John Ericsson Memorial: "Memorials and Monuments" scrapbooks, Washingtoniana Division, D.C. Public Library. William J. Wheatley, "Ericsson Statue Beset by Delays: Selection of Site Was Held Up Pending Adoption of Bridge Plans," *Evening Star*, May 30, 1926. "President and Swedish Prince Honor Ericsson at Memorial Unveiling," *Washington Post*, May 30, 1926.

Cuban Friendship Urn: "Have You Seen This Monument?," *Washington City Paper*, May 24, 1996. "Urning Their Keep," *Washington City Paper*, May 31, 1996. "Cuban Friendship Urn to Be Rededicated," *Washington Post*, June 13, 1998.

Tidal Basin: Mary Kendall Shipe, Historic American Engineering Record, Tidal Reservoir Outlet, HAER No. dc-9-b, 1988. "Walsh Would End Tidal Basin Beach," *Evening Star*, February 18, 1925.

# BIBLIOGRAPHY

Books:

Allen, William C. *History of the United States Capitol: A Chronicle of Design, Construction, and Politics.* 106th Cong., 2nd Sess., 2001. S. Doc. 106–29. Washington, D.C.: U. S. Government Printing Office, 2001.

Barber, Lucy G. *Marching on Washington: The Forging of an American Political Tradition.* Berkeley and Los Angeles: University of California Press, 2002.

Bedford, Steven McLeod. *John Russell Pope: Architect of Empire.* New York: Rizzoli, 1998.

Bedini, Silvio A. *The Jefferson Stone: Demarcation of the First Meridian of the United States.* Frederick, Md.: Professional Surveyors Publishing Company, 1999.

Bowling, Kenneth R. *The Creation of Washington, D.C.* Fairfax, Va.: George Mason University Press, 1991.

Bryan, Wilhelmus Bogart. *A History of the National Capital.* 2 vols. New York: Macmillan Company, 1914–16.

Burger, Barbara Lewis, comp. *Guide to the Holdings of the Still Picture Branch of the National Archives.* Washington, D.C.: National Archives and Records Administration, 1990.

Chapell, Gordon. *East and West Potomac Parks: A History.* Denver, Colo.: National Park Service, 1973.

Collins, Kathleen. *Washingtoniana: Photographs.* Washington, D.C.: Library of Congress, 1989. A detailed guide to the photographs relating to Washington, D.C., at the Library of Congress.

Conaway, James. *The Smithsonian: 150 Years of Adventure, Discovery, and Wonder.* New York: Alfred A. Knopf; Washington, D.C.: Smithsonian Books, 1995.

Concklin, Edward F. *The Lincoln Memorial in Washington.* Washington, D.C.: Government Printing Office, 1927.

Crouch, Tom D. *The Eagle Aloft: Two Centuries of the Balloon in America.* Washington, D.C.: Smithsonian Institution Press, 1983.

Dowd, Mary-Jane M., comp. *Records of the Office of Public Buildings and Public Parks of the National Capital.* Washington, D.C.: National Archives and Records Administration, 1992. A guide to the records of this office and its predecessors held by the National Archives.

Field, Cynthia R., Richard E. Stamm, and Heather P. Ewing. *The Castle: An Illustrated Guide to the Smithsonian Building.* Washington, D.C.: Smithsonian Institution Press, 1993.

Goode, George Brown, ed. *The Smithsonian Institution 1846–1896: The History of Its First Half Century.* Washington, D.C.: Smithsonian Institution, 1897.

Goode, James M. *Capital Losses: A Cultural History of Washington's Destroyed Buildings.* Second Edition. Washington, D.C.: Smithsonian Books, 2003.

Goode, James M. *The Outdoor Sculpture of Washington, D.C.* Washington, D.C.: Smithsonian Institution Press, 1974. A second edition is forthcoming

Grooms, Thomas B. *World War II Memorial.* Washington, D.C.: U.S. General Services Administration, 2004. A detailed history of the memorial, distributed free at the dedication ceremony.

*Guide to the Smithsonian Archives.* Washington, D.C.: Smithsonian Institution Press, 1996.

Gutheim, Frederick, and Antoinette J. Lee. *Worthy of the Nation: Washington, D.C., from L'Enfant to the National Capital Planning Commission.* Baltimore, Md.: Johns Hopkins University Press, 2006.

Halprin, Lawrence. *The Franklin Delano Roosevelt Memorial.* San Francisco, Calif.: Chronicle Books, 1997. The *Washington Post*, April 27, 1997, contains several useful articles on the memorial.

Heine, Cornelius. *A History of the National Capital Parks.* U.S. Department of the Interior, 1953.

Henry, Robert S. *The Armed Forces Institute of Pathology: Its First Century 1862–1962.* Washington, D.C.: Office of the Surgeon General, Department of the Army, 1964. A history of the Army Medical Museum.

Hines, Christian. *Early Recollections of Washington City.* 1866. Reprint. The Junior League of Washington, 1981.

Jacob, Kathryn Allamong. *Testament to Union: Civil War Monuments in Washington, D.C.* Baltimore, Md.: Johns Hopkins University Press, 1998.

Keim, De Benneville Randolph. *Keim's Illustrated Hand-book. Washington and its Environs: A Descriptive and Historical Handbook to the Capital of the United States of America.* Washington, D.C., 1874, 1888 (rev. eds.). A guidebook to Washington, with detailed descriptions of the sights on the Mall.

Kite, Elizabeth S. *L'Enfant and Washington.* Baltimore, Md.: Johns Hopkins Press, 1929.

Kohler, Sue A. *The Commission of Fine Arts: A Brief History 1910–1995.* Washington, D.C.: Commission of Fine Arts, 1996.

Kohler, Sue A., and Pamela Scott, eds. *Designing the Nation's Capital: The 1901 Plan for Washington, D.C.* Washington, D.C.: U.S. Commission of Fine Arts, 2006.

Kopper, Philip. *America's National Gallery of Art: A Gift to the Nation.* New York: Harry N. Abrams, 1991.

Lawton, Thomas. *Freer: A Legacy of Art.* Washington, D.C.: Freer Gallery of Art, Smithsonian Institution, 1993.

Lessoff, Alan, and Christof Mauch, eds. *Adolf Cluss, Architect: From Germany to America.* New York and Oxford: Berghahn Books, 2005.

Longstreth, Richard, ed. *The Mall in Washington, 1791–1991.* Washington, D.C.: National Gallery of Art, 1991. A collection of articles on various aspects of the Mall, focusing on architectural history and city planning.

Mackintosh, Barry. *The United States Park Police: A History.* Washington, D.C.: Department of the Interior, 1989.

Mills, Nicolaus. *Their Last Battle: The Fight for the National World War II Memorial.* New York: Basic Books, 2004.

Moore, Charles. *Daniel H. Burnham: Architect, Planner of Cities.* Boston and New York: Houghton Mifflin Company, 1921.

Moore, Charles. *The Life and Times of Charles Follen McKim.* Boston and New York: Houghton Mifflin Company, 1929.

Myer, Donald Beekman. *Bridges and the City of Washington.* Washington, D.C.: The Commission of Fine Arts, 1974.

Oehser, Paul H. *The Smithsonian Institution.* Boulder, Colo.: Westview Press, 1983. A history of the Smithsonian Institution.

Park, Edwards, and Jean Paul Carlhian. *A New View from the Castle.* Washington, D.C.: Smithsonian Institution Press, 1987. About the Smithsonian Quadrangle Project.

Peterson, Jon A. *The Birth of City Planning in the United States, 1840–1917.* Baltimore, Md.: Johns Hopkins University Press, 2003.

Rathbun, Richard. *The Columbian Institute for the Promotion of Arts and Sciences.* Washington, D.C.: Government Printing Office, 1917.

Reiff, Daniel D. *Washington Architecture 1791–1861: Problems in Development.* Washington, D.C.: U.S. Commission of Fine Arts, 1971. Contains a chapter "James Renwick and A. J. Downing in Washington."

Reps, John W. *Monumental Washington: The Planning and Development of the Capital Center.* Princeton, N.J.: Princeton University Press, 1967. A history of Washington's monumental core, focusing on the McMillan Plan.

Reps, John W. *Washington on View: The Nation's Capital Since 1790.* Chapel Hill, N.C.: The University of North Carolina Press, 1991. A large-format book that tells the history of Washington's monumental core through maps and prints.

Scott, Pamela. *Capital Engineers: The U.S. Army Corps of Engineers in the Development of Washington, D.C. 1790–2004.* Alexandria, Va.: Office of History, Headquarters, U.S. Army Corps of Engineers, 2005

Scott, Pamela. *Temple of Liberty: Building the Capitol for a New Nation.* New York: Oxford University Press, 1995. An architectural history of the Capitol through the mid-nineteenth century, with an epilogue on the later extensions.

Scott, Pamela, and Antoinette J. Lee. *Buildings of the District of Columbia.* New York: Oxford University Press, 1993. Covers each of the most architecturally significant buildings in the city; includes an essay on the history of the Mall.

Solit, Karen D. *History of the United States Botanic Garden, 1816–1991.* Washington, D.C.: Government Printing Office, 1993.

Spreiregan, Paul, ed. *On the Art of Designing Cities: Selected Essays of Elbert Peets.* Cambridge, Mass.: MIT Press, 1968. Includes essays on the Lincoln Memorial and nearby sculpture.

Thomas, Christopher A. *The Lincoln Memorial and American Life.* Princeton, N.J.: Princeton University Press, 2002.

Torres, Louis. *"To the Immortal Name and Memory of George Washington": The United States Army Corps of Engineers and the Washington Monument.* Washington, D.C.: Government Printing Office, 1984.

U.S. Arlington Memorial Bridge Commission. *The Arlington Memorial Bridge.* 68th Cong., 1st Sess., 1924. S. Doc. 95. Washington, D.C.: Government Printing Office, 1924.

U.S. Army Corps of Engineers. *Annual Report of the Chief of Engineers to the Secretary of War,* 1867–1923. Includes annual reports of the Office of Public Buildings and Grounds, which detail improvements to the Mall.

U.S. Commission of Fish and Fisheries. *Annual Report of the Commissioner of Fish and Fisheries,* 1881–1903.

U.S. Congress. House of Representatives. *Documentary History of the Construction and Development of the United States Capitol Building and Grounds.* 58th Cong., 2nd Sess., 1904. H. Rept. 646. Washington, D.C.: Government Printing Office, 1904.

U.S. Congress. House of Representatives. *Report of the Thomas Jefferson Memorial Commission.* 75th Cong., 1st Sess., 1937. H. Doc. 367. Washington, D.C.: Government Printing Office, 1937.

U.S. Congress. House of Representatives. *Report of the Thomas Jefferson Memorial Commission.* 75th Cong., 3rd Sess., 1938. H. Doc. 699. Washington, D.C.: Government Printing Office, 1938.

U.S. Congress. House of Representatives. Committee for the District of Columbia. *Investigation Into the Affairs of the District of Columbia.* 42nd Cong., 2nd Sess., 1872. H. Rept. 72. Contains information on the filling of the canal.

U.S. Congress. Senate. Committee on the District of Columbia. *Report of the Senate Committee on the District of Columbia on the Improvement of the Park System of the District of Columbia.* 57th Cong., 1st Sess., 1902. S. Rept. 166. Washington, D.C.: Government Printing Office, 1902. Better known as the McMillan Plan.

U.S. Congress. Senate. Committee on the District of Columbia. *The Mall Parkway, Hearing . . . March 12, 1904, on the Bill (S. 4845) Regulating the Erection of Buildings on the Mall, in the District of Columbia.* Washington, D.C.: Government Printing Office, 1904.

U.S. National Capital Park and Planning Commission. *Annual Report of the National Capital Park and Planning Commission,* 1927–1932.

Wearmouth, John. *The Pope's Creek Branch.* Washington, D.C.: National Railway Historical Society, 1986. Covers the Baltimore and Potomac Railroad.

Weller, Charles F. *Neglected Neighbors.* Philadelphia, Pa.: John C. Winston Co., 1909. Describes Louse Alley.

*The WPA Guide to Washington, D.C.* New York: Pantheon Books, 1983. Reprint of *Washington, D.C.: A Guide to the Nation's Capital.* New York: Hastings House, 1942.

Yochelson, Ellis Leon. *The National Museum of Natural History: 75 Years in the Natural History Building.* Washington, D.C.: Smithsonian Institution Press, 1985.

Yonkers, Tescia Ann. *Shrine of Freedom: Thomas Jefferson Memorial,* 1983. A pamphlet on the Thomas Jefferson Memorial with information on the sculpture by Rudulph Evans.

ARTICLES:

Beauchamp, Tanya Edwards. "Adolph Cluss: An Architect in Washington During the Civil War and Reconstruction." *Records of the Columbia Historical Society* 48 (1971–72): 338–358.

Belanger, Dian Olson. "The Railroad in the Park: Washington's Baltimore & Potomac Station, 1872–1907." *Washington History* 2, No. 1 (Spring 1990): 4–27.

Binczewski, George J. "The Point of a Monument: A History of the Aluminum Cap of the Washington Monument." *JOM* 47 (November 1995): 20–25.

Bowling, Kenneth R. "From 'Federal Town' to 'National Capital': Ulysses S. Grant and the Reconstruction of Washington, D.C." *Washington History* 14, No. 1 (Spring/Summer 2002): 8–25.

Canty, Donald. "Masterful Placemaking Beside the Mall." *Architecture* 76 (November 1987): 42–49. About the Smithsonian Quadrangle Project.

Capasso, Nicholas J. "Vietnam Veterans Memorial." In *The Critical Edge: Controversy in Recent American Architecture*, edited by Tod A. Marder, 189–202. Cambridge, Mass.: MIT Press, 1985.

Dudar, Helen. "New Treasures on the Mall." *Smithsonian* 18 (September 1987): 44–63.

Fish, Marilyn B. "East Building, National Gallery of Art." In *The Critical Edge: Controversy in Recent American Architecture*, edited by Tod A. Marder, 75–86. Cambridge, Mass.: MIT Press, 1985.

Forgey, Benjamin. "For Art's Sake." *Washington Post Magazine*, April 11, 1993. About renovations to the Freer Gallery of Art.

Hawkins, Don A. "The City of Washington in 1800: A New Map." *Washington History* 12, No. 1 (Spring/Summer 2000): 74–77. The entire issue is devoted to the early years of Washington, D.C.

Hawkins, Don A. "The Landscape of the Federal City: A 1792 Walking Tour." *Washington History* 3, No. 1 (Spring/Summer 1991): 10–33.

Heine, Cornelius. "The Washington City Canal." *Records of the Columbia Historical Society* 53–56 (1953–56): 1–27. The definitive account of the canal.

"Improvement of Potomac Flats, Washington." *Scientific American* 65 (September 19, 1891): 180–181. A description of how the dredging and filling was accomplished.

Jeffers, Thomas C. "The Washington Monument: Various Plans for Improvement of Its Surroundings." *Landscape Architecture* 39 ( July 1949): 157–163.

Judge, Joseph. "New Grandeur for Flowering Washington." *National Geographic Magazine* 131 (April 1967): 500–539.

McNeil, Priscilla W. "Rock Creek Hundred: Land Conveyed for the Federal City." *Washington History* 3, No. 1 (Spring/Summer 1991): 34–51. Covers the original proprietors of the L'Enfant city and their holdings, including a new map.

Meisler, Stanley. "Sculpture Blossoms in a New Garden on the Mall." *Smithsonian* 30 (August 1999): 62–67. About the National Sculpture Garden.

Rhees, William Jones. "Reminiscences of Ballooning in the Civil War." *The Chautauquan* 27 ( June 1898): 257–262.

Schmertz, Mildred F. "Underneath a Garden." *Architectural Record* 175 (September 1987): 112–121. About the Smithsonian Quadrangle Project.

Scott, Pamela. "Robert Mills and American Monuments." In *Robert Mills, Architect*, edited by John M. Bryan, 143–177. Washington, D.C.: The American Institute of Architects Press, 1989. The Washington Monument and its architect.

*SOM News*, No. 57 (August 1966). An article by John M. Woodbridge on the SOM Plan fills the issue.

Taft, William Howard. "Washington: Its Beginning, Its Growth, and Its Future." *National Geographic Magazine* 27 (March 1915): 221–292. Includes color reproductions of renderings made for the McMillan Commission, updated to 1915.

Thomas, Christopher A. "The Marble of the Lincoln Memorial: 'Whitest, Prettiest, and . . . Best.'" *Washington History* 5, No. 2 (Fall/Winter 1993–94): 42–63. An overview of the memorial and its architect.

MISCELLANEOUS:

Fanning, Kathryn. "American Temples: Presidential Memorials of the American Renaissance." Ph.D. dissertation, University of Virginia, 1996. Covers the memorials to Grant, Lincoln, and Jefferson in Washington; the proposed memorial to Theodore Roosevelt on the Tidal Basin; and several memorials outside Washington.

KressCox Associates, *Historic Structures Report: Tidal Basin Inlet Bridge, Washington, D.C.* Washington, D.C.: 1986.

Lowry, Bates, ed. *The Architecture of Washington, D.C.* 2 vols. Washington, D.C.: Dunlap Society, 1976–1979. Microfiche containing reproductions of more than 3,500 photographs and architectural drawings held by various institutions.

Office of the Curator [of the Capitol]. "Nineteenth Century Fences on the Capitol Grounds." Office of the Curator of the Capitol. Photocopy, 1986.

Papi, Lara. "History of the National Aquarium." The National Aquarium. Photocopy, n.d.

Robinson and Associates, Inc. "East and West Potomac Parks Historic District: Revised National Register of Historic Places Nomination." 1999.

Skidmore, Owings and Merrill. "Washington Mall Circulation Systems. Prepared for the National Park Service, Department of the Interior," 1973. The 1976 Development Plan, available at the National Capital Region Headquarters of the National Park Service.

Skidmore, Owings and Merrill. "The Washington Mall Master Plan," 1966. The 1966 SOM Plan, available at the National Capital Region Headquarters of the National Park Service.

U.S. Commission of Fine Arts. Minutes [of monthly meetings]. Commission of Fine Arts. Typescript, 1910–.

U.S. Congress. Senate. *Message of the President of the United States . . . relative to the mall in the city of Washington, and the selection of the site of an armory thereon.* 34th Cong., 1st Sess., 1856. S. Doc. 88. Summary of the legislative history of the Mall, with some additional information, by Secretary of War Jefferson Davis.

U.S. Department of the Interior. National Park Service. "Final Environmental Statement, Proposed Rehabilitation of the National Mall, Third Street to Fourteenth Street, Madison Drive to Jefferson Drive, Washington, D.C." [1975].

U.S. National Capital Park and Planning Commission. "Minutes of the 81st meeting of the National Capital Park and Planning Commission . . . October 20–21, 1933." National Capital Planning Commission. Typescript, 1933.

Very useful are Washington newspapers, especially the *Daily National Intelligencer,* the *Evening Star,* and the *Washington Post.* See also the vertical files at the Washingtoniana Division of the D.C. Public Library; the Historical Society of Washington, D.C.; and the Smithsonian Institution Archives. Especially helpful are the Internet websites of the Architect of the Capitol, Library of Congress, Smithsonian Institution, National Gallery of Art, and National Park Service. The documentation of the Historic American Buildings Survey and the Historic American Engineering Record at the Prints and Photographs Division of the Library of Congress are also available on the Internet.